THE
CITIZEN
HOUSEWIVES'
GUIDE

3rd Impression

Published by the "Evening Citizen," Ltd.
: 195 Albion Street, Glasgow, C.1 :

CONTENTS

FOREWORD

House-keeping, at one time, was regarded as a very fine art indeed. A woman trained for it then as she might train now for teaching or secretarial work.

House-keeping is still a great art. But nowadays it is an art which a woman is expected to fit in with scores of other daily tasks. The word " housewife " no longer only describes a married woman with a family.

Perhaps you are one of the countless married women who has a whole or part-time job. Perhaps you are a single woman working nine-to-five and keeping a home going (yes, and being your own handyman, too!).

You, too, then, are one of the housewives—the practical, versatile housewives—for whom this Guide has been planned.

You don't like cooking? Margaret Little has written about it in a way that will make it more interesting for you. If you are a beginner, she explains and describes the things you want to know. If you are an experienced cook, you will still find that she can give you some useful " wrinkles."

Washing and cleaning are not glamorous or exciting jobs. But this Guide will help you to do them more quickly, more efficiently. It will make them seem less tiresome.

First aid, infectious diseases, flower arrangement, baby care—the versatile housewife is expected to know something about all of them. In this Guide, authoritative writers deal fully with these and many other subjects.

The Guide has been designed in this handy shape and size so that you can keep it near you in the kitchen. You will find there are blank pages in it. These have been left so that you can write or paste into them all the special items that you will want to keep as they appear daily in the Housewives' Page of the " Evening Citizen."

Instead of a stack of loose cuttings, you will have the items and recipes where you want them, when you want them.

Our aim in the Housewives' Club will be to bring back some of the interest and fun and skill which should all be a part of house-keeping. It's fun to try out something new, even if it's only a different way of making scones or a different colour of cushion for an armchair. It's interesting to find a quicker and better way of doing a dreary job. And it takes real skill to plan your spending so that there is money for the odd, small luxury.

Welcome to this Housewives' Club!

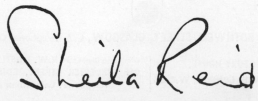

Women's Editor.

Cookery *by*

MARGARET LITTLE

WHAT TO BUY FOR YOUR KITCHEN:

What is the best equipment for a kitchen? There is no need for anything too elaborate but buy the best you can afford. It is economy in the long run.

Beginning from scratch, the following **LIST** will be helpful:—a clock: set of measuring spoons: two graduated measures: bowls: vegetable and chopping knives: grater: steamer: spatula: potato peeler: pastry cutters: patty tins: cake tins: flour and sugar sifters: wooden spoons: set of sauce-pans with lips: ordinary sauce-pans with lids: double boiler: fireproof dishes: tin opener: cork screw: bread knife: nylon sieve: small and large frying pans: frying basket: pastry board: baking sheet: girdle: scales: jelly pan: pudding moulds: chopping board: meat saw.

Guides to Quantities and Measures:

Most of us get tied in knots at times when tackling a recipe which needs to be translated from tablespoons to ounces, and from cups to gills. Success will not come without accurate weighing and measuring.

HANDY MEASURES are useful to know and save a lot of time. It is worthwhile having the following table for reference:—

Dry Measure—All Level Spoons

    1 saltspoon=¼ teaspoon
    4 teaspoons=1 tablespoon
    2 tablespoons flour=1 ounce
    2 tablespoons sugar=1½ ounces
    2 tablespoonfuls breadcrumbs=½ ounce
    1 small teacup flour=4 ounces
    1 small teacup sugar=6 ounces
    1 medium sized egg=2 ounces

Liquid Measure

    8 tablespoonfuls=1 gill=5 ounces
    1 small teacup=1 gill
    2 gills=½ pint
    4 gills=1 pint

He also learns much who studies himself.

Oven heat, too, is often another worry and yet why should it be? Modern stoves are all so much easier to regulate than old-fashioned ones. Most **GAS** ovens are controlled thermostatically. The numerals or letters on the indicator remove the necessity for guessing the required heat. Set the indicator head to give this, leave for 15 minutes and the oven is ready for use. And, thanks to the **THERMO-STAT**—a mechanical thinking machine—this heat remains steady all the time.

But perhaps **OVEN HEAT** is specified in Degrees, what then? The following **TABLE** should be helpful as it shows the various readings in variety. It is understood, of course, that the best position for the temperature indicator is to have the shelf about half-way up the oven. Put the shelf in position when lighting the oven.

Broadly speaking, too, for **SLOW** cooking, choose a shelf near the foot and for **QUICK** cooking, a shelf near the top.

ELECTRIC OVENS generally show temperatures and for these the following table may be applied. A pilot light fades out to show when the " setting " temperature is reached.

If there is no pilot—allow 15 minutes heating up before using the oven.

Letter	Number	Approx. Temp.	Description	Example
A.	¼—1	250ºF	Very Slow	Meringues
B. & C.	2—3	300ºF—325ºF	Slow	Baked Custard
D.	4	350ºF	Very Moderate	Biscuits
E.	5	375ºF	Moderate	Sponge Sandwich
F. & G.	6—7	400ºF—425Fº	Fairly Hot	Bread
H.	8	450ºF	Hot	Rich Pastry
J.	9	475ºF		
K.	10	500ºF	Very Hot	Browning Off
L.	11	525ºF		

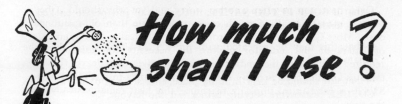

How much shall I use?

Standard proportions are good to know and even for the most experienced cooks they save a lot of looking-up time.

Milk Puddings

1½ ozs. cereal per 1 pint milk; with barley and whole rice allow 2 ozs.

Blanc Mange

2 ozs. cereal per 1 pint milk; with barley and whole rice allow 3 ozs

Custard

Baked: Allow 2 eggs per pint milk.

Steamed: Allow 4 eggs per pint milk.

Jellies

1½ to 2 ozs. gelatin per 2 pints liquid.

BASIC INGREDIENTS

Creams

½ oz. gelatin per pint liquid.

Suet Puddings

1 lb. farinaceous food, 8 oz. suet, 4 to 6 ozs. dried fruit.

Cake Mixture

1 egg, its weight in margarine and sugar, 2½ ozs. flour, pinch of baking powder.

Sauces

¼ pint liquid, 1 oz. cooking fat, 1 oz. flour.

Plain Buns

1 lb. flour, 4 ozs. fat, 2 teaspoons baking powder.

Biscuits

6 ozs. flour, 4 ozs. margarine, 3 ozs. sugar.

Hints for Cook

DO YOU KNOW?

—that a spoonful of vinegar added to the water in which a **FOWL** is boiled will make the bird more tender.

—that tough or coarse **MEAT** soaked in vinegar and oil—1 part vinegar, 2 parts oil—has a better flavour, and that tough **MEAT** rubbed with vinegar before cooking is often more tender.

—that **LEMONS** packed in salt and not touching each other will keep in good condition for several weeks.

It is never too late to mend.

—that if **SOUP IS TOO SALTY,** thick slices of raw potato cooked in it till tender will draw some of the salt.

—that this may be repeated with more **POTATOES** and then the potatoes used, too.

—that salt should be kept in a dry place; that a pinch of salt added to **COFFEE** just before serving brings out the flavour.

—that a little salt sprinkled on the roasting tin *before* roasting a joint gives the gravy a better flavour.

—that when cutting apples for tarts or salads dropping the slices into cold salted water—1 teaspoon salt per pint water—prevents discolouring; and that they should be rinsed in fresh water before using.

—that when **ONIONS** are needed for **SAVOURIES** it is quicker to grate than to chop them and the flavour comes out more strongly.

—that **MEAT** can be easily **BASTED** in the oven if you tie a piece of fat in some muslin and hang this from an oven grid above the meat.

—that **BREAD** will brown at once when you fry it if you first put it under the **GRILL** for a few minutes.

—that **JAM JARS** won't crack when you are filling them if you stand each jar on a steel knife as the hot jam is poured in.

—that **NEW POTATOES** will be easier cleaned if soaked first in cold water and salt.

—that **CLOTHES PEGS** are useful for clipping muslin to a bowl when liquid is being strained through it.

—that if **BARLEY** is shaken in a strainer before washing, it removes some of the flour and makes it much easier to wash.

—that **STALE BREAD** put through the mincer with sultanas and dates and toasted very slowly at the bottom of the oven makes a tasty addition to a breakfast cereal.

—that **CRUSHED CEREAL** makes a very good topping for a macaroni dish.

—that **PINK-COLOURED ICING** can be made without cochineal. Add a little red jelly along with the icing sugar and hot water. It improves the flavour, too.

—that **LENTILS** or **SPLIT PEAS** will cook much quicker if they are not soaked but simply washed and added to hot stock.

—that a **LEMON** will keep fresh longer if a segment is cut out and replaced each time after juice has been squeezed from the lemon.

—that one or two finely crushed **BUTTERSCOTCH** or **RUSSIAN TOFFEES** sprinkled on top of a baked milk pudding a few minutes before taking it from the oven will give it a delicious candy flavour.

—that a dessertspoon of **VINEGAR** added to the water in which old potatoes are boiled will help prevent them turning black.

A fault confessed is half redressed.

—that **SYRUP** or **TREACLE** will be more easily spooned if you first dip the spoon in boiling water.

—that a little warm **SYRUP** brushed over **APPLE** or **RHUBARB TARTS** when they come out of the oven will give them a professional finish.

—that you can measure half-a-cup of **FAT** by half-filling the cup with water and adding enough fat to bring the water to the top.

—that **FAT** can be easily rubbed into **PASTRY** if you grate it through a flat cheese grater, at the same time scooping up the flour with the block of fat.

—that **MINT LEAVES** will chop more quickly if they are first sprinkled with a little sugar.

—that **DOUGHBALLS** will cook easily and lightly if you lay them on greaseproof paper on top of the mince in the pot.

Roasting Hints

Cooking times are often difficult to assess, but the following guides should help. (For each case assume 4 lb. to 6lb. joints).

Home-Fed Beef: 15 minutes per pound and 15 minutes over.

Rolled Roast: 20 minutes per pound and 20 minutes over.

Stuffed: 25 minutes per pound and 25 minutes over.

Chilled Beef: Must be thawed thoroughly before cooking. If the joint is **HARD** leave it in a warm place for 2 to 3 hours—then give 25 minutes per pound and 25 minutes over.

Home-Fed Mutton and Lamb: 20 minutes per pound and 20 minutes over.

Stuffed or Stuffed and Rolled: 25 minutes per pound and 25 minutes over.

Chilled Mutton and Lamb: 25 minutes per pound and 25 minutes over.

Pork: 25 minutes per pound and 25 minutes over.

GRILLING HINTS

Heat the grill pan well before using; and have the grill red hot. Best thickness for **STEAK** is 1½ to 2 inches thick; **CUTLETS** and **CHOPS**—the thickness of the bone. Any doubt about "tenderness" beat steak or cutlet on both sides with the back of a wooden spoon. Before grilling, rub all over surface with oil or a little butter. Turn meat frequently during cooking to prevent "dryness."

BEEFSTEAK is best underdone. **MUTTON** and **LAMB** must be fully cooked.

When cooking is almost complete sprinkle over a little seasoning.

FRYING

Heat fat gradually and never let it burn.

Keep the fat at "smoking" point while articles are being fried.

Dry surface of foods to be fried before putting into the fat and apply a "coating" if necessary. If a wire basket is used heat it in the fat before putting the food into it. This prevents sticking.

Do not fry too much at a time. This means reduced temperature of fat—which makes the food indigestible.

Drain fried food on crushed up "bakers' bags" on removal from pot. Re-heat fat between each batch. Strain fat through muslin after use—to keep it clean and free from food particles.

A friend's frown is better than a fool's smile.

Pastry Making

Rules to Remember:

1. Use any kind of fat—margarine, lard, dripping, butter. If a mixture is used instead of only one variety, work the fats slightly together before adding them to the flour.
2. Cut the fat into the flour with a knife, before using your fingers.
3. Add only sufficient water to give the correct consistency. When adding water, always add it to the dry part of the mixture.
4. Cool pastry dough before using—this allows for shrinkage.
5. Handle little and lightly when rolling.
6. Bake pastry in a hot oven—the richer the pastry the hotter the oven.

Using 8 ozs. Flour:

Kind of Pastry	Prop. of Fat.	Method of Adding	Oven Heat	Uses
Short	4 ozs. margarine	Cutting and Rubbing	425°F	Sweet and Savoury
Rough Puff	5 to 6 ozs. margarine and lard or margarine only	In lumps to flour then by rolling and folding	450°F	Sweet and Savoury
Flaky	6 ozs. margarine and lard or margarine only	By rolling and folding	460°F	Sweet and Savoury
Puff	8 ozs. margarine	For 1 Part— then rolling and folding	475°F	Sweet and Savoury
Suet	3 ozs. suet and ½ teaspoon Baking Powder	Rubbing in	450°F or Steamed or Boiled	Sweet and Savoury

Nothing is troublesome that we do willingly

Short Pastry:

8 ozs. flour, pinch salt, 4 ozs. margarine, cold water to mix. Sift together flour and salt. Cut and rub in fat till mixture resembles fine breadcrumbs. Add cold water and work to a stiff consistency. Turn on to a floured board. Knead well till smooth. Roll once and use as required for sweet or savoury dishes.

Rough Puff Pastry:

8 ozs. flour, 6 ozs. margarine, 1 teaspoon salt, squeeze lemon juice, cold water. Sift flour and salt. Add the fat in walnut-sized pieces. Mix in with a knife. Make a well in the centre of the flour and add lemon juice and enough cold water to make an elastic dough. Turn on to a floured board. Work lightly and roll in a 4 ins. wide strip about 12 ins. long. Flour lightly, fold in three, give a half-turn so that the open ends are to and from you. Roll again, fold and repeat five times in all. Use as required.

Flaky Pastry:

8 ozs. flour, 1 teaspoon salt, 6 ozs. margarine and cooking fat (mixed), squeeze lemon juice, cold water to mix. Work fast together.

 Divide into four parts, equal in size. Cut and rub one part into sieved flour. Add salt; add lemon juice to cold water (about $\frac{1}{4}$ gill). Mix to an elastic dough. Turn out on to a board and work lightly. Roll out into a strip. Arrange one part of the fat down two-thirds of the strip in small pats, flour lightly, fold in three, give a half-turn and roll out again. Continue in same way with rest of fat. Give five rollings in all. Use as required.

Puff Pastry:

8 ozs. flour, pinch salt, 8 ozs. margarine, cold water, squeeze lemon juice. Press fat lightly in corner of floured cloth to soften. Sieve flour and salt. Mix to an elastic dough with lemon juice and cold water. Knead on a floured board till smooth. Roll out into a square. Place pat of fat in the centre and fold dough over it—to make a neat parcel. Roll out into a narrow strip—keeping the open ends to and from you. Dust with flour—brush this off and fold in three. Roll out again. Repeat seven times in all, setting the dough aside for 20 to 30 minutes between every two rollings. Use as required.

Suet Pastry:

8 ozs. flour, 3 to 4 ozs. chopped suet, $\frac{1}{2}$ teaspoon salt, 1 teaspoon baking powder, about 1 gill cold water. Sieve flour. Mix together all dry ingredients. Rub suet into flour with finger tips. Mix with cold water to an elastic consistency. Turn on to a floured board. Roll once and use as required.

Study not to beautify thy face but thy mind.

B

FOOD PRESERVATION

By this the cook means to keep food fit for human consumption for longer than would naturally be the case. There are different ways of doing this and here are some of them:—

EGGS

To store eggs successfully the pores of the shell must be sealed and there are many ways of doing this. If you have limited storage space use this method:

Lard and Boracic

Mix together 2 ozs. lard and 1 to 2 ozs. boracic acid. Smear the eggs with this and wrap in a greaseproof paper. Store in a strong box in a dark, cool place, and cover to keep out dust. Keep some extra mixture and use it as more eggs become available. Quantities given are sufficient for 7 to 8 dozen eggs.

FRUIT BOTTLING

Both jam jars with suitable lids and special jars made for the purpose may be used. Have the fruit firm and ripe. Grade it for size and ripeness when washing. Prepare according to kind and pack tightly into the jars. For covering liquid use cold water or a syrup (4 to 6 ozs. sugar and 1 pint water) Boil it up. Strain through muslin. Cool and use.

Apply heat—using the oven or a pan for sterilizing.

Oven. Temperature, 300°F. for 1¼ hours or until fruit changes colour, and the skin cracks.

Pan. This must have a false bottom and a tight fitting lid. Pour cold water in to come to shoulder of bottles.

Cooking. Bring to simmering point in 1¼ hours. Hold this temperature for 10 to 15 minutes.

Cooling. Put jars in a cool place away from draughts.

Testing. Next day test for seal, which must be perfect.

Storage. Keep in a cool, dark, dry cupboard.

HERBS are generally dried. Pick them on a dry day and before the sun has beaten down on them.

LARGE LEAVED HERBS. Wash and shake well. Pick off leaves and spread them on a muslin covered cooling tray. Dry slowly in the oven and when crisp rub them down with the fingers and store in a tightly covered jar.

SMALL LEAVED HERBS are tied in bundles and hung up till dry, when they are easily rubbed down and stored as above.

JAMS and **JELLIES, CHUTNEYS** and **PICKLES** are other ways of making sure that summer and autumn fruits and vegetables are " saved " for the dark winter days. All jams consist of acid+pectin+ sugar in the correct proportion and jam lacking in pectin will not set.

Violent passions lead to great depressions.

Pectin is in the skin cell walls and pips of the fruit and acid helps to extract it.

The fruit is simmered gently to draw the pectin out *before* the sugar is added. Fruits rich in pectin and acid make very easily into jam. Very ripe fruit is not recommended because during ripening the pectin becomes pectic acid which will not form a " gel."

As well as drawing out the pectin, acid improves colour and flavour and helps to prevent sugar crystalizing and for a good " gel " this is essential. If acid is known to be lacking it **must** be added, and there are several ways of doing this:—

1. **Lemon Juice**—about 2 tablespoons to 2 pounds fruit.
2. **Fruit Juice** (from fruits rich in pectin)—about ½ pint to each 4 pounds fruit.
3. **Citric Acid**—a small teaspoon to 2 pounds fruit; too much causes the jam to " weep."

Sugar is important for many reasons. Without enough sugar there is a poor " gel," the flavour is poor, and the jam won't keep.

Sugar is a preservative but too much will spoil the fruity flavour of the jam and encourage crusting crystalization.

Average Proportion of Sugar is 1 pound to 1 pound fruit. There are exceptions, of course. Fruits lacking in acid and pectin need less sugar—12 ozs. sugar to 1 pound fruit; and fruits rich in acid and pectin need more sugar—18 to 20 ozs. per 1 pound fruit.

The Type of Pan is Important. A thick one is best to prevent burning and to lessen the chance of fruit sticking. Before starting, rub a little butter over the bottom of the pan.

Scum is inevitable in jam making: just skim it off. It does no harm apart from encouraging mould and spoiling the appearance.

In **Jelly making** only the fruit juice is used with sugar. Therefore, you must have two boilings. Use any weight of fruit for the **first boiling.**

Fruit and water are simmered together to extract the pectin and acid. When pulpy it is all strained through a jelly bag or double cheese cloth and left to drip.

Water. No accurate measurements can be stated. After the fruit has been washed and prepared, put it into a pan and **almost cover** with cold water.

Pectin. You can find the amount of this in the fruit juice by mixing 1 teaspoon of cold juice and 3 teaspoons methylated spirit. A jelly-like clot should form at once. If it does not or is very weak, there is too much water, and the remedy is to boil up the juice again to reduce the quantity. Then re-test and, when satisfactory, measure the juice and add accurately measured sugar.

For a Strong Clot—1 to 1¼ pounds sugar to each pint of juice.

For a Medium Clot—12 ozs. sugar to each pint of juice.

I recommend you to try the above test because by knowing what the clot is like you will get much more accuracy and save a lot of time and heat.

Never put off until tomorrow what you can do today.

4 famous PAISLEY LABELS

"GOLDEN SHRED"

ROBERTSON'S BRAMBLE SEEDLESS FULL FRUIT STANDARD

SILVER SHRED LEMON MARMALADE SPECIAL STANDARD

Robertson's MINCE MEAT "GOLDEN SHRED" BRAND

Preserves of the highest
standard made by
Robertson's of Paisley
Established 1859

Holders of the Institute of
Hygiene Certificate since 1907

For the **second** boiling: Boil up measured fruit juice. Add measured sugar and stir till boiling. Boil up without stirring to setting point—generally about 15 minutes. Test for setting—let a little cool on a saucer. When a skin forms on top—at once remove the scum. Fill the jelly into warm, dry jars without delay. Do not let it cool before potting.

MARMALADE AND JAM

Unrationed sugar means that you no longer have to hoard for several months in order to stock up your shelves with jams, jellies and marmalade.

Marmalade making is easy, though novices are sometimes afraid to attempt it. For them, the following hints should be helpful.

1. Scrub the fruit before using.
2. Allow 3 pints of water to each pound fruit.
3. Soak pulp, peel and water for 24 hours before cooking. This lessens the time for the first boiling as it helps to soften the pectin.
4. Two boilings are necessary: the first, pulp and water (about 1 hour); the second, pulp and sugar.
5. Most of the pectin is found in the pith and pips and these must be soaked and boiled with the pulp.
6. Tie the pips loosely in muslin and if you don't want the pith in the marmalade, cut it up roughly and tie with the pips.
7. Before the second boiling remove the muslin bag, squeezing any pectin clinging to it.
8. Although oranges are rich in acid, so much water is used, the proportion is relatively small and lemon juice is often added.
9. Do not overcook with the sugar.
10. Boil quickly to setting point and allow to cool in the pan until a skin begins to form on the surface. Stir up and pot. This prevents skin and solid parts from rising to the top of the jars.

THICK MARMALADE (about 13 lbs).

Two pounds **BITTER ORANGES,** 2 **LEMONS,** 2 **SWEET ORANGES,** 6 pints **WATER, SUGAR** (about 6½ lbs.).

Wash the fruit, halve and remove pips. Put them in a basin and cover with water. Shred the fruit very finely and soak 24 hours with the water. Empty pulp into a jelly pan. Add strained liquid from the pips and also the pips tied in muslin.

Boil up and cook one hour or until the peel is soft. Empty all into a basin and leave 24 hours. Measure the pulp, boil up and add sugar —1¼ lbs. to each pint of pulp. Dissolve this, then boil quickly to setting point. Skim, cool, pot, cover and store.

BLACKCURRANT JAM (about 7 lbs.)

Two pounds clean **BLACKCURRANTS,** 2 pints **WATER,** 3½ lbs. **SUGAR,** ½ oz. **BUTTER.**

Simmer the currants gently about 20 minutes in water until soft. Add the sugar and dissolve carefully. Boil fast to setting point—about 15 minutes. Test. Add butter and stir until melted to scatter any scum and break it down. Cool well and pot.

Judge not that you be not judged.

CHUTNEY

A good chutney is smooth and mellow. It needs long, slow cooking in a lined pan which prevents any chemical action between acid ingredients and metal.

Have a strong pan so that there is less danger of sticking, and a wooden spoon, and if sieving is necessary use a monel metal or nylon sieve.

Store the chutney in a cool, dry, and preferably dark cupboard. Have the jars dry and warm before use. Pot the chutney at boiling point and put on the waxed tissues at once.

" Sealing " chutney is not of first importance. Chutney keeps under a jam pot cover, but it will shrink quite a bit. With a patent lid there is very little shrinkage. If metal lids are used, make sure that the waxed tissues are large enough to completely cover the chutney. It is recommended that chutney is stored for at least six weeks after making and before using. The chutney will be more mellow and the flavour better.

When making chutney use spiced vinegar in preference to plain varieties. This can be bought, but it is easily made at home. Here is a good recipe for:—

Spiced Vinegar:

1 quart vinegar, $\frac{1}{2}$ oz. cinnamon stick, $\frac{1}{2}$ oz. Jamaica peppercorn, $\frac{1}{2}$ oz. clove stalks, $\frac{1}{2}$ oz. whole mace. Tie the spices in muslin and put into a lined sauce-pan with the vinegar. Bring slowly to boiling point. Remove pan from heat. Cover with a plate and leave until quite cold. The infusion is then complete. Lift out the spice bag. Bottle the vinegar and use as required. It will keep indefinitely.

Tomato Chutney:

3 pounds tomatoes, 6 ozs. sugar, 1 heaped teaspoon salt, pinch of cayenne pepper, 1 saltspoon paprika pepper, 1 tablespoon Tarragon vinegar, 1 cup spiced vinegar. Wash tomatoes. Put in a basin and well cover with boiling water. Leave for one minute. Pour off boiling water and cover with cold water (this makes them easier to handle). Peel, quarter tomatoes, cutting out the hard cores. Simmer them gently in a pan until thick and pulpy. Add the other ingredients and simmer slowly until thick. Pot and cover as detailed above.

Sweet Pickles are popular. They are very heavy on the sugar, but a few jars might be put down to be used on a special occasion as a treat. The foundation is **Vinegar Syrup.** The fruit is carefully cooked in this without breaking down and pulping it. Then it is packed gently into warm, dry jars and, after **slight reduction** to an " oily " consistency boiling syrup to cover is poured over. It is sealed and stored six weeks before use.

Vinegar Syrup:

1 pint white vinegar, $1\frac{1}{2}$ pounds brown sugar, 1 teaspoon ground cloves, 1 teaspoon Jamaica pepper, 1 teaspoon ground cinnamon. Mix spices and sugar. Put vinegar into a lined pan. Add sugar and dissolve. Boil up. Add selected fruits and cook until tender without breaking down. Continued as directed above.

Knowledge makes you humble.

PICKLES:

Home pickling is easy and fascinating, and if you have a garden with more vegetables than you can use—preserve some of them as pickles. You need:—

1. Fresh vegetables.
2. Brine (1 pound salt dissolved in 1 gallon cold water).
3. Spiced vinegar.
4. Jars for storing.
5. Paraffin wax for sealing.

Prepare the vegetables according to their type. For example: cucumber, peel and cube; French Beans, wash, " string " and slice; Cauliflower, wash and break into sprigs; Small onions, peel and leave whole; larger ones, peel and cut into slices.

Put all prepared vegetables into a crock or basin. Cover with brine and leave for 48 hours. If necessary, weigh them down to keep them completely immersed. Lift out. Drain well and wash to remove all traces of salt.

Drain to remove excess water, and pack into dry jars, to within one inch of the top. Cover well with cold spiced vinegar. **Dry round inside neck of jars.** Carefully pour on melted paraffin wax to seal completely. Draw the wax over the rim of the jars with the finger. Store for six weeks before using.

Little deeds are like little seeds.

WHEN YOU *Plan* YOUR KITCHEN, CHOOSE
`ENGLISH ELECTRIC`
DOMESTIC APPLIANCES

It's a hundred times easier if all those
appliances are made by *one* firm.   With 'ENGLISH ELECTRIC'
domestic appliances you can do this with complete confidence.
'ENGLISH ELECTRIC' manufacture a full range of domestic
appliances uniform both in looks and quality, each one
the finest in its field.

H.P. TERMS. *'ENGLISH ELECTRIC' Domestic Appliances are obtainable on
attractive Hire Purchase terms from your Electricity
Service Centre or Authorised 'ENGLISH ELECTRIC' Dealer.*

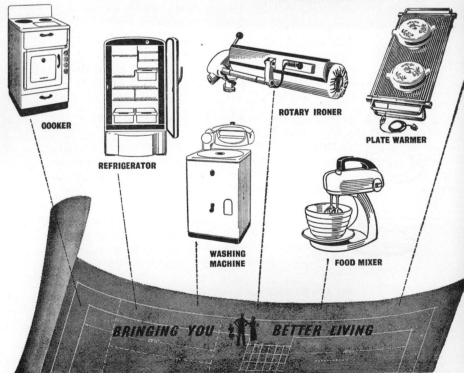

COOKER

REFRIGERATOR

ROTARY IRONER

PLATE WARMER

WASHING MACHINE

FOOD MIXER

BRINGING YOU BETTER LIVING

The ENGLISH ELECTRIC Company Limited, Domestic Appliance Division, East Lancashire Road, Liverpool, 10

Hygiene

To keep flies away put a bunch of mint in a jam jar with water in the kitchen, or hang a bunch of nettles from the ceiling.

Hygiene means a constant war against Bacteria and Dirt. It is good for the housewife to set herself a high standard of cleanliness, for that is the easiest way to fight the tiny organisms which destroy foods and harm human beings.

The following rules are good to remember:—

1. Keep the kitchen clean and tidy.
2. Dispose of refuse quickly and use a covered container.
   (See that this is emptied daily and wash with disinfectant.)
3. Have good ventilation and good light.
4. Have clean towels for drying your hands, when you wash them frequently—and become clean food conscious.

The purer the food, the more liable it is to infection and contamination. These foods, therefore, must have special attention.

MILK: Keep this in as cool a place as possible, and certainly away from sunlight. Stand the bottles in a large basin of cold water with handful each of salt and washing soda added. See that the bottles are covered with muslin or plastic caps.

Scald milk jugs daily with boiling water and do not dry the inside.

BUTTER: Keep this in an earthenware container, or cooler, which can be bought very cheaply, or put it on a plate, cover it with muslin and put an upturned flower pot over it.

CHEESE: Wrap it in muslin or greaseproof paper. You can make double sure of it by soaking the muslin in vinegar and hanging it up with the cheese in it, or wrap cheese in aluminium foil.

MEAT: Whether raw or cooked, it must be kept away from dust and flies. Don't partially cook it one day and finish the cooking the next day. If you haven't a fridge, dust the meat lightly with pepper or rub it with vinegar and then cover it with a wire cover or a piece of muslin.

He that promises too much means nothing.

FISH: Cook fish as soon after purchasing as possible. Always buy shell fish alive.

Wash all Meat and Fish before cooking. Dry it with **CLEAN** muslin **KEPT** for the purpose and remember, **MUSLIN** used for this purpose and for covering must be scalded frequently.

GREENS: These should be bought fresh as you need them so that you get their full goodness. They will keep crisp for a few days if stored in a pan with a tight fitting lid.

ROOTS:

Keep these on a rack. Don't have anything on the floor.

SOUR MILK

If you do have sour milk don't throw it out. There are so many ways of using it—in salad cream for scone making, or as . . .

Crowdie:

1 quart thick sour milk, 1 oz. margarine, pinch salt. Collect the sour milk for a day or two. It must be thick for Crowdie. Heat it but do not boil it. Lift off the curd as it comes to the surface. Tie it in butter muslin, hang it on a nail and let it drip overnight. Beat a little margarine into this curd and add salt to taste. Spread on scones or oatcakes.

Sour Milk Scones:

2 teacups flour, 1 small teaspoon each cream of tartar and baking soda, 1 level teaspoon salt, $\frac{1}{2}$ oz. lard, about 1 cup sour milk. Mix dry ingredients. Sift. Rub in fat. Stir in enough milk to make an elastic dough. Use a knife for mixing. Turn on to a well floured board and knead lightly. Roll into a round $\frac{1}{2}$ inch thick. Cut into four and place on a hot girdle. When lightly browned turn and bake until cooked through and the edges quite dry.

Stir-About Pudding:

2 teacups flour, good pinch salt, 1 rounded teaspoon each baking soda and mixed spice, 1 egg, 1 tablespoon each syrup and sugar, 2 ozs. each margarine and lard, 2 apples, sour milk. Sieve the dry ingredients and cut and rub in fats. Add syrup to beaten egg. Add this with coarsely grated apples (skins on) to the flour mixture. Stir in enough milk to make a dropping consistency. Turn into a greased basin and cover with greased paper. Steam $1\frac{1}{2}$ to 2 hours. Serve with custard sauce.

Never cross a bridge until you come to it.

CARE OF HOUSEHOLD ¦EQUIPMENT

No matter how energetically you dust and sweep around the house you will never get the best results unless your household equipment is kept as it ought to be.

VACUUM CLEANERS and **ELECTRIC POLISHERS**: These should be emptied at once after use. They cannot work efficiently if they are clogged. Loop the cable neatly. It is worth paying to have the maker service the machine regularly, oiling and adjusting it. If a plug seems slack or faulty, have it seen to at once.

CARPET SWEEPERS deserve good attention, too. They will not work properly if the brush is wrapped round with threads and hairs. Keep the brush clear and see that the rubber " bumpers " are in the proper places. Keep the wheels smoothly oiled. And always empty the box after use.

BRUSHES should be regularly washed in soapy ammonia water, rinsed, and hung bristles downward to dry. This includes hearth and boot brushes. Put a piece of string round sweeping brush handles so that they can be hung up when they are not in use.

MOPS must be clean and free from grit or they will scratch the the floors. Shaking a mophead out of a window is the least satisfactory way of getting rid of dust. Rather cover the head with an old bit of flannel which is easily washed when dirty.

DUSTERS must be regularly washed and **FLOOR CLOTHS** should be washed through and hung up outside occasionally.

DISH MOPS and **CLOTHS** need as much attention as **DISH TOWELS.** They should be regularly boiled to keep them absolutely clean.

Nothing is impossible to a willing heart.

*British Biscuits
at their Best*

Macfarlane Lang

ESTABLISHED 1817

By Appointment
Biscuit Manufacturers
to the late King George VI
Macfarlane Lang & Co., Ltd.

Housewives' Hints

A pinch of bicarbonate of soda added to **MILK** in hot weather will keep it from turning sour.

BURNED -SAUCEPANS can be easily cleaned if a dessertspoonful of bicarbonate of soda and a pint of cold water is placed in them and slowly brought to the boil.

When **CLEANING PICTURES,** fix a slice of cork at the lower edges of the back of the picture. This prevents dust collecting and prevents the picture marking the wallpaper.

To clean a **DUST-BIN,** burn some newspapers or straw in it each time it is emptied.

PEWTER need be cleaned only once or twice a year. Dip a cloth in whitening and sweet oil and polish well

Valuable **VASES** are best filled with some sand or shot to keep them from being easily knocked over.

When a coat collar or felt hat has become greasy or marked, rub it with eucalyptus oil.

At the first sign of a **COLD** breaking out on the lips, dab it at once with vinegar.

Keep your **ELECTRIC BULBS** clean by occasionally covering them with a paste made from bicarbonate of soda and cold water. Smear this on the glass and let it dry. Sponge it off later with soapy water. It will remove brown stains and give a brighter light.

A little **FLOOR POLISH** mixed to a soft cream with turpentine and rubbed with a soft cloth on to lino will give it a high polish.

Save old **NEWSPAPERS,** bore a hole through the lot of them and hang them on a string beside the kitchen sink. Use them to wipe all greasy plates and pans. It saves dirtying cloths and the papers are useful afterwards for setting fires.

Collect ends of **SOAP** in an empty muslin flour bag and use it on wash days.

If **BOTTLES** are too narrow to clean by hand, crush up an egg shell and shake it around in the bottle with hot water.

ALUMINIUM pans should be cleaned with steel wool and never with soda.

Use soda and hot water for cleaning **CAKE TINS.** Dry thoroughly before storing.

Our last garment is made without pockets.

TILES will keep clean longer if wiped with paraffin after washing.

If the **CHIMNEY** goes on fire throw salt on the fire, shut door and windows of the room and hang a soaking wet cloth over the front of the fireplace.

Most dirty and greasy spots in **CARPETS** are easily removed if rubbed vigorously with eucalyptus oil.

HEAT MARKS on polished surfaces are difficult to remove, but camphorated oil rubbed on vigorously with cotton wadding may do the trick.

To keep a **BED** from getting damp, even if left for two or three weeks, leave a blanket on top of it after it is made. Air this blanket before using it again.

A **SMALL MIRROR** placed between the **SHEETS** will betray a damp BED by going misty if left in for a few minutes.

A handful of soda in a disused aluminium saucepan will clean **SILVER** boiled in it for half an hour or more; rinse the silver in hot soapy water, and polish.

A two pound jar of lime will keep a small **DAMP LARDER** or pantry dry and sweet.

Equal parts of vinegar and water should be used to clean **GILT FRAMES.**

Salt in washing water will prevent coloured **CLOTHES** from running or fading.

Liquid ammonia applied with an old toothbrush will remove verdigris from brass **TAPS.**

Brown boot polish is excellent for leather **UPHOLSTERY,** but be sure there is none left on to mark clothes.

To clean an **ENAMEL BATH** scour well with a tablespoonful of dry kitchen salt and a little turpentine, then wash with warm soapy water.

ENAMELLED FURNITURE should not be washed with soap or soda but should first be cleaned with methylated spirits then, at once, washed with tepid water that has a little fine oatmeal in it. Rub in paraffin oil and polish with a clean duster.

To make a cloth for cleaning **SILVER** add a teaspoonful of plate powder and a tablespoonful of ammonia to a cup of water (or more if necessary) and saturate cloth in it and allow to dry.

WET BOOTS and **SHOES** should be packed with paper to absorb moisture and retain shape. Drying by heat will make them crack and perish.

A good rubbing with turpentine will clean **SUEDE SHOES,** but hang them to dry in a current of air till the smell goes. New emery paper is good, too.

Better a fortune in a wife than with a wife.

CARROTS will cook quicker if a little fat is added to the water.

Shrivelled **LEMONS** can be made plump, juicy and fresh again if they are put into cold water, which is then brought to the boil.

To make a **CAKE** turn out easily, place the tin on a damp cloth for a few minutes after removing it from the oven.

A **BAKED CUSTARD** will not curdle if the dish is put into a tin of cold water before setting it in the oven.

When **POACHING EGGS** add a teaspoon of vinegar before dropping in the eggs to ensure successful setting.

To make **LIVER** more tender when frying, dip it first in milk and then in flour.

To keep **FISH** fresh overnight, lay it on an ashet, cover with a piece of clean, damp paper and sprinkle the paper thickly with salt.

To kill the smell when cooking **CAULIFLOWER** or **CABBAGE** put a fairly thick slice of bread in the pan.

Add a few drops of vinegar or lemon juice to the water when boiling rice to keep the **RICE** white, and help to separate the grains.

When weighing **SYRUP**, sprinkle the scales with flour and the syrup will roll off.

To preserve any **EGG YOLK** not used with the white, pour a little cold water over it, cover, and put in a cool, dark place.

When beating **EGGS** and **SUGAR** for sponges, it is much quicker to beat the eggs well before adding the sugar and whisking again.

To curl **BRANDY SNAPS** after baking, roll them round the oiled handle of a spoon.

SUET DUMPLINGS will be much lighter if boiling water instead of cold water is used for mixing.

A few drops of vanilla added to **MASHED DATES** when making sandwiches gives a delicious caramel flavour.

When sewing loops on **KITCHEN TOWELS** make them of elastic instead of tape. Then when you wipe your hands in a hurry you won't tear the towel from its hook.

When **PAINTING WINDOWS** rub a turpentine rag over the glass. Any paint spots will then be easily removed.

An old **HOT WATER BOTTLE** filled with clean rags or soft paper will make a useful kneeling mat for gardening or household.

Rub **MIRRORS** all over with dry soap and polish with a soft cloth. This keeps them from steaming over.

Revenge is the only debt which it is wrong to pay.

"Surely you do too?"

Surely you use Domestos for your lavatory as a *safe* protection from germs. Thousands of Hospitals and Nursing Homes do. Domestos gets clean round the unseen bend — *without* a brush. Domestos keeps everything sweet and spotlessly clean.

Price 1/1d. plus 2d. on bottle.

DOMESTOS

The Brushless Lavatory Cleanser

STAINS

All stains should be treated as quickly as possible. Use the simplest methods first. If you are using a special fluid and the fabric is delicate, first test it, if possible, on an unseen piece of the material.

GREASE STAINS ON A CARPET: Stain should be sprinkled at once with whiting or flour. Repeat this next day and rub with a flannel dipped in turpentine.

COD LIVER OIL stains must be treated before washing the garment. Place the stain over a saucer and pour over some carbon tetrachloride. Let the stain soak in this for a little, then rub with a white rag. Wash in hot, soapy water.

DYES sometimes spread from one garment to another when being washed. Treat with methylated spirit with a small quantity of ammonia added to it.

FRUIT STAINS should be treated with borax and warm water. If this fails try rubbing with half a lemon dipped in salt, then wash as usual.

INK STAINS will often yield to cold water. Alternatively, use peroxide or lemon juice.

MILK STAINS should be washed first with cold then hot water.

Soak **EGG STAINS** in cold water before laundering.

Sponging with warm water will often remove **JAM** marks, but if any colour remains, rub with borax and warm water.

BLOOD STAINS: A little starch should be mixed and spread on the stain, allowed to remain for a few hours, then wash.

PAINT should be treated with paraffin working from the outside edge inwards.

HOT PLATE marks should be treated with a few drops of methylated spirits worked well into the wood with a pad of cotton wool. Polish with a soft rag.

To remove **SEA-WATER** stains from brown leather shoes, rub with a solution made by dissolving a small lump of washing soda in two tablespoons hot milk. Apply with a rag and repeat when dry. Clean with ordinary shoe polish.

STAINS ON LEATHER: Remove by rubbing the leather dipped in spirits of wine.

Be a friend to virtue, a stranger to vice.

Electrolux *Excels* in Reliability

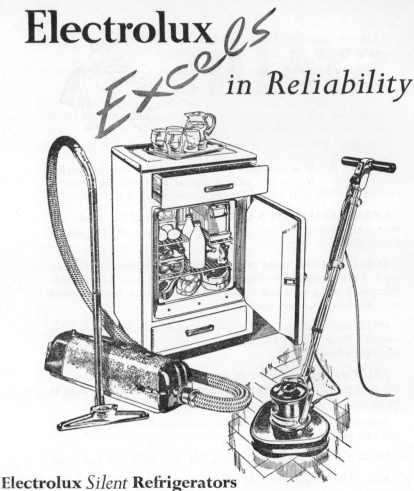

Electrolux *Silent* **Refrigerators**

made history 30 years ago and have since become world famous. The original refrigerator without machinery or moving parts with all the improvements and refinements evolved during 30 years of experience and constant research. Models—1½ to 7 cu. ft.—*silently* operated by Gas, Electricity, Paraffin or Bottled Gas. *Cooling Unit is guaranteed for 5 years.*

Electrolux *Quiet* **Home Cleaner**

Quietly . . . gently . . . it extracts all the dust, not merely from carpets but from all furnishings, too. Tools for floor-to-ceiling cleaning (without extra cost) make Electrolux more than a carpet cleaner. *2- Year-Guarantee.*

Electrolux *Quiet* **Floor Polisher**

excels in speedy, effortless polishing of parquet, marble, tiled, lino and other flooring — *quietly,* without disturbance. Triangular body gets right into corners. Triple-brush action — originated by Electrolux 25 years ago — ensures effortless one-hand control. *2-Year-Guarantee.*

Electrolux Ltd
153-5 Regent Street · London W.1
5 Wellington Street · Glasgow

By Appointment
Refrigerator Makers
to the late King George VI

By Appointment
Suction Cleaner and
Refrigerator Manufacturer
to the late Queen M

GRASS stains should be rubbed with methylated spirits then washed.

Moisten **MILDEW** stains and rub in finely powdered chalk before washing.

And—a useful tip to remember when you are washing a stained article—run a fast coloured thread round the stain so that you can easily spot the area and give it a special rub when it is wet.

IODINE STAINS: Rub the stain with a freshly-cut lemon. Or, dab with a sponge dipped in ammonia diluted with water until the stain disappears.

IRON MOULD: Cover the stain with salt and then squeeze a few drops of lemon juice on top. Leave for half an hour and then rinse in a weak solution of ammonia and wash in clean water.

PERSPIRATION STAINS: Place the garment in warm water containing a little ammonia—do not use soap. Allow to soak for half an hour. If stain has not entirely disappeared, squeeze a little lemon juice on it and rinse in clean warm water.

RUST STAINS: Chop a clean stalk of rhubarb and boil it in a cup full of water until the water is reduced by half. Boil the stained portion in this solution for quarter of an hour. Moisten white material with lemon juice then spread it with salt. Leave it until the stain disappears, then wash.

TEA STAINS: Tea stains on china can be removed by salt rubbed on the china when damp. Tea stains on table linen: Soak the stained material in a solution consisting of half a teaspoonful of borax to a cupful of water. Then rinse in boiling water. Alternatively, apply lemon juice and expose to the sun for a few days.

COFFEE STAINS: Wash with soap and hot water and dry in the sun. Or, a little glycerine should be gently rubbed on the stain, rinse in tepid water, and iron on the wrong side. Or, mix the yolk of an egg with a little warm water and use as a soap on the stain.

COCOA or **CHOCOLATE STAINS:** Soak in cold water softened with a little borax. Then stretch the stained part over a basin and pour boiling water through the stain.

STAIN ON A METAL TEAPOT: Put a tablespoonful of baking soda into the teapot, fill with cold water and put on the range, let it boil for three minutes. Pour out the water and wash with clean suds then rinse.

INK STAINS IN A CARPET: If the stain is still wet cover thickly with salt and remove with a spoon, applying fresh salt until no more ink is absorbed. Then rub the spot with a cut lemon and rinse with clean water.

TAR STAINS: Sponge stain with turpentine and rub well. Wash in hot soapy water and rinse. Ordinary metal polish will also remove the tar.

SOOT STAIN ON A CARPET: If soot falls on a carpet cover it at once with dry salt and sweep it up carefully. If a mark is still left rub the spot with a rag dipped in carbon tetrachloride.

Wilful waste makes woeful want.

A good word is as soon said as an ill one.

HOUSEWIVES' HINTS—NOTES

Be not the first to quarrel with a friend.

Laundering

In this climate few housewives are rash enough to buy anything without first asking "Will it wash?" Knowing the correct method to use for each different fabric can mean the difference between failure and success.

If you are doubtful about colours being fast, make this simple test: lay a damp white handkerchief over a piece of the hem. If a fair amount of colour transfers to the handkerchief when pressed with a hot iron the colour is not fast. If there is a faint tinting, the garment can still be washed by itself in cool water with soapflakes and rinsed quickly.

The following list is a guide to treating different materials.

WOOL: Wash in lukewarm, creamy lather. Squeeze the garment but don't soak, rub or wring. Don't hold it up so that it stretches with its own weight. Rinse two or three times in cool water. Roll in a towel and dry away from the heat. Press when dry under a damp cloth.

COTTON and **LINEN:** These can stand boiling. Iron damp with a hot iron.

CORDUROY, VELOUR and **VELVET:** Wash in hot, soapy water. Don't attempt to wring after rinsing but hang dripping on a line. Brush up the pile with a soft cloth as it dries.

SILK: Wash in the coolest possible water. Dry away from direct heat and press while damp with a warm iron.

RAYON: Use lukewarm water and do not twist or wring—it is weakest when wet. Iron slightly damp with a moderately hot iron. Sprinkling with water to dampen will leave patchy marks. If necessary, rinse the whole garment again.

RAYON GABERDINE: Wash in rich, lukewarm lather, squeezing gently. Don't wring or twist. Rinse twice in water of similar heat and roll in a towel to remove as much water as possible. Iron on the reverse side with a moderately hot iron.

RAYON JERSEY: Wash in lukewarm soapy water and dry flat to keep the shape. Press when damp with a warm iron, being careful not to stretch the hem.

CREPE: Wash in lukewarm water. Iron when nearly dry with a cool iron, pulling the fabric out to shape.

SHANTUNG, TUSSORE: Wash in lukewarm soapy water. Iron on reverse side when bone dry with a warm iron.

A good example is the best sermon.

DUPION: Squeeze in lukewarm soap flakes. Iron when slightly damp on the reverse side with a warm to moderately hot iron.

BRODERIE ANGLAISE and **COTTON ORGANDIE:** Squeeze in hand-hot lather. Iron damp with a moderately hot iron on the reverse side.

COTTON SEERSUCKERS and **CRIMPS:** Squeeze in hand-hot lather. When quite dry, press the double sections—collar, pocket flaps —lightly.

EVERGLAZE: Wash in warm, soapflake lather. Iron damp on the right side with a moderately hot iron. You can be sure that glazed fabrics won't run—only fast colours will take on a glaze.

NYLON and **TERYLENE:** Wash in soapy water as hot as the hand can stand. Never boil nylon. Most nylon fabrics, except seersucker, look the better of pressing lightly with a cool iron. They will dry with fewer creases if you hang them dripping wet over a basin or bath.

LACE: Wash in lukewarm soapy water, handling gently. Roll in a towel to remove as much water as possible. If a lace fabric shrinks, iron slightly damp with a moderately hot iron, stretching gently. To make it crisp, use a light starch. Fragile old lace should be tacked on muslin and washed in a warm, frothy lather. Lace collars can be washed by shaking in a jam jar of warm, soapy water.

INDIANA COTTON RAINCOATS: Scrub lightly with a clean, soapy nailbrush. Dry with a clean cloth and hang in a cool place.

RUBBERISED RAYON and **SATIN RAINCOATS:** Sponge off mud marks with warm, soapy water. Wipe over with a clean, damp cloth. Dry away from direct heat.

HOME FURNISHINGS

BLANKETS: Use three tablespoons of soap flakes to a gallon of lukewarm water and work the blankets gently in this lather. Don't rub. Rinse three times in lukewarm water (it is important with woollen articles to have washing and rinsing waters of the same heat). Hang stretched across two clothes lines to allow the air to circulate. Shake the blanket occasionally.

WASHABLE EIDERDOWNS: Gently press up and down for three minutes in a rich lather. Rinse three times, forcing the water through the feathers but without wringing. Peg by the four corners on to a double line and shake occasionally when drying.

Rash promises are ill to keep

LOOSE COVERS: Slubbs, repps, brocades, cretonnes and rayons can all be washed in a lukewarm lather. First shake thoroughly and brush the piping with a stiff brush. Use a soapy brush in the water for very soiled parts. Rinse and dry outside. Cottons and linens look the better of a light starching. Iron when nearly dry, then replace on the furniture. Finish off there with the iron.

CANDLEWICK BEDSPREADS: Wash in a good lather but don't wring. Press out the surplus water and dry in a breeze, if possible. Shake as it is drying and a final shaking when quite dry will bring up the fluff.

LAMPSHADES: Stitched silk and rayon shades can be washed in lukewarm flakes, rinsed, shaken and patted with a towel. Dry with tissue paper between the metal frame and the fabric to prevent rusting. Parchment and vellum shades can be sponged with a clean cloth wrung out in soapy water.

TABLECLOTHS and **TABLE MATS:** Wash in a warm lather. Iron embroidered parts on reverse side on a thick, soft pad. Seersucker cloths should be pressed lightly.

NET CURTAINS: Roll net, lace, marquisette or ninon curtains loosely and tie with tapes. This will prevent them pulling out of shape or tearing. Rinse in plain, cold water first, then soak for a little while in lukewarm suds. Rinse well, open out and dry, if possible, on stretchers. Iron when slightly damp, stretching gently, except at the edges.

Riches serve a wise man but command a fool.

WALLPAPER

The regulation "piece" or roll of wallpaper is 21 inches wide and 36 feet in length. In wallpapering, one piece in ten is allowed for waste in matching patterns, etc. The following table gives number of pieces required for rooms of varying measurements:

Feet round Room	HEIGHT OF ROOM								
	7 to 7½ feet	7½ to 8 feet	8 to 8½ feet	8½ to 9 feet	9 to 9½ feet	9½ to 10 feet	10 to 10½ feet	10½ to 11 feet	11 to 11½ feet
28	4	4	4	4	5	5	5	5	5
29	4	4	4	5	5	5	5	5	6
30	4	4	5	5	5	5	5	6	6
31	4	4	5	5	5	5	6	6	6
32	4	4	5	5	5	6	6	6	6
33	4	5	5	5	5	6	6	6	6
34	4	5	5	5	6	6	6	6	7
35	5	5	5	5	6	6	6	7	7
36	5	5	5	5	6	6	6	7	7
37	5	5	5	6	6	6	7	7	7
38	5	5	6	6	6	7	7	7	7
39	5	5	6	6	6	7	7	7	7
40	5	5	6	6	6	7	7	7	8
41	5	6	6	6	7	7	7	8	8
42	5	6	6	6	7	7	7	8	8
43	6	6	6	7	7	7	8	8	8
44	6	6	6	7	7	7	8	8	8
45	6	6	7	7	7	8	8	8	9
46	6	6	7	7	7	8	8	8	9
47	6	6	7	7	7	8	8	9	9
48	6	6	7	7	8	8	8	9	9
49	6	7	7	7	8	8	9	9	9
50	6	7	7	8	8	8	9	9	9
51	7	7	7	8	8	8	9	9	10
52	7	7	7	8	8	9	9	9	10
53	7	7	8	8	8	9	9	10	10
54	7	7	8	8	9	9	9	10	10
55	7	7	8	8	9	9	10	10	10
56	7	7	8	8	9	9	10	10	10
57	7	8	8	9	9	9	10	10	11
58	7	8	8	9	9	10	10	11	11
59	8	8	8	9	9	10	10	11	11
60	8	8	8	9	9	10	10	11	11

Pardon all but thyself.

SPOTLESS WASHING

THE WHITE BOIL : Put your dry white articles into cold Surf suds, and bring to the boil. But if the water is hot, as it would be for a second load, be sure that stained garments are rinsed through cold water first or stains may become set. There's no need to boil for more than a few minutes. Rinse first in hot and then in lukewarm water. You'll see the difference right away when you boil in Surf. Surf is the complete detergent designed specially to give you a spotless boil. Even stubborn stains vanish — leaving everything more than just white — spotless.

THE WHITE WASH : If you prefer not to boil, Surf's rich, penetrating suds still give you the whitest wash. Just wash clothes through in hot Surf suds; Surf lathers instantly — rich lather that lasts throughout the wash.

COLOUREDS : The following instructions are for fast-coloured cottons and linens that are not suitable for boiling with the white wash. Squeeze through in hand hot Surf suds. Only the extra grubby places need to be rubbed gently. Rinse well, first in hot water, then in cold. Hang up to dry immediately, and if you dry outdoors, don't hang them in strong sunlight. If colours are not fast, wash separately and quickly in lukewarm suds. Surf gives you really sparkling coloureds. It removes all trace of dirt and grime quickly and gently, so that the true colours come up radiant and fresh as new.

THE FINE WASH : All your fine things are safe in Surf — silks, rayons, nylon and wool too — they'll all be fresh, sweet and really clean when washed in Surf. Make sure colours are fast, and then just squeeze your clothes through lukewarm Surf suds. Surf gently lifts out every speck of dirt.

HOUSEHOLD CLEANING : Surf cleans everything spotless — quicker and easier. Use Surf for washing up — Surf suds simply make grease vanish. Just rinse and leave to dry: no need to wipe — dishes, glasses and cutlery all sparkle. Use it round the house for enamel, porcelain, tiles and taps: also for paintwork, floors, windows and carpets. Yes, Surf does all your household jobs.

A *LEVER* PRODUCT

A spotless boil, a spotless wash, Surf — the complete detergent

Be your own Valet

Whether you spend a lot or a little on clothes, you ought to give them that little bit of care which will keep them looking smart. Many times you may have admired a woman—or a man—who was not at all strikingly dressed but had a very **WELL-GROOMED LOOK.**

The first good rule is—never delay in making **REPAIRS** or removing **STAINS.** All clothes should be left out to air after being worn. But before you put them in the wardrobe, check on those stains or repairs. Certain stains, if left, become firmly fixed and then need to be sent to the cleaners.

Wardrobe mistresses with big touring companies have the unenviable job of keeping scores of dresses looking as fresh as new for months on end. And when they have to deal with stains they advise: " Use **FRESH WATER** or **SOAPY WATER** before trying anything stronger."

Instead of rubbing the fabric very hard and possibly spoiling the pile, put a pad of towelling under the material and soak the stain with water, pressing it in gently.

FOOD STAINS can usually be moved without difficulty if you tackle them at once. A little ammonia in the water is good for greasy stains.

Shake your clothes when you take them off and **BRUSH** them with a stiff brush. And remember to give the brush an occasional wash.

It pays to have a good many **COATHANGERS.** Do up the fastenings of skirts and jackets and hang skirts from hooks rather than slinging them over bars.

Tighten any **BUTTONS** or do any repairs to hems or linings before you put the garments away. It is no use hanging anything in your wardrobe unless it is ready for wear the minute you want it.

If you have white **COLLARS** or **CUFFS** on a dress or suit, make sure that it removes for easy washing. To be really efficient, have a spare set which can be tacked into place as you remove the soiled ones.

WINTER COATS usually collect much more dirt than can be removed with a clothes brush. Put the upholstery attachment on to the vacuum cleaner and run this over them occasionally.

Know thyself.

You'll feel far better off with Sunfresh in the home

JUST ORANGES

IN A

BOTTLE

Sunfresh

REGISTERED TRADE MARK

**JOSEPH DUNN (Bottlers)
LTD. GLASGOW, S.E.**

Mothercraft

Mothercraft is not, unfortunately, something that every woman instinctively knows. All mothers have to learn the correct handling of a child, the correct methods of feeding, the things that can go wrong and the signs that arc alarming but are not, in fact, serious. Some of these can be learned only from experience. Others are matters of common-sense and care.

STERILIZATION of **FEEDING BOTTLES** and **TEATS** is one of the most important things to be learned in caring for a baby. Bottles have to be rinsed with the most scrupulous care prior to boiling otherwise an invisible film of milk will harden inside and make a refuge for germs.

To make a proper job of sterilizing, you need the following equipment:—

A **GLASS** or earthenware **DISH** to hold 2 pints water.

A **TABLESPOON** or **MEASURE**.

A small **GLASS** or meat paste **JAR**.

A bottle of household **ANTISEPTIC**.

A soapless **DETERGENT** (your chemist will advise you which is the most suitable).

After feeding your baby, rinse the outside of the teat and the bottle under the cold tap before removing the teat.

Remove the **TEAT** and rinse inside it and inside the bottle under the cold tap. Take a bottle brush and the soapless detergent and very thoroughly rinse the bottle to remove all traces of milk film. Rinse in cold water two or three times.

He hath no leisure who useth it not.

Put the bottle, teat and the glass jar into water containing the anti-septic (usual quantity is **1 TABLESPOON ANTISEPTIC** to **2 PINTS WATER).** Cover the teat with the glas jar to keep it under water. See that no air bubbles remain in either teat or bottle. Leave in this solution until the next feed.

Before preparing the feed, wash the **HANDS** thoroughly and then remove the bottle, teat and glass from the antiseptic solution. Rinse the bottle and pour in the food. Keep the teat covered in the glass jar until ready to put it on.

Provided the antiseptic solution is kept away from dust it need only be renewed once every **24 HOURS.**

When your baby goes on to a more **VARIED DIET,** you will have to have a lot of patience with him at meal times.

Never try to rush a meal. When **SPOON FEEDING,** baby will try to hold the spoon and this will make everything slower—and messier. Spread a good area of plastic cloth around him so that you don't have to worry about carpets or tablecloth. The more he handles the spoon himself, the sooner he will learn to feed himself.

DON'T FUSS over him too much. Remember that his training now is setting the pattern for his table behaviour in the future.

If he is not at all anxious to feed from a spoon, try him with a **SMALL CUP** instead.

Between 12 and 14 months begin brushing his **TEETH** with a small soft brush. Teeth should be brushed up and down, not across the mouth.

Nearly all young mothers are alarmed by any appearance of a **RASH** or **SPOTS.** Yet these sometimes have a very simple explana-tion. The following are some ailments common in young children:—

SCURF: Scales show on the scalp. Make sure that all soap is rinsed away after washing.

GUM RASH: A rash of bright red spots appears on the face and later spreads to the body. It is caused by teething and an upset digestion. Soothe the spots with bicarbonate of soda lotion and give a very mild laxative.

THRUSH: This is usually caused by unclean feeding bottles and is shown by greyish patches in the baby's mouth. These must be gently removed with a clean piece of lint soaked in boracic lotion before and after each feed. After cleansing, smear a little glycerin of borax over the inside of the cheeks and on the tongue. Everything used in the preparation of baby's food must be rigorously cleaned.

NAPKIN RASH: Baby's buttocks and thighs will look red and inflamed and the skin may even blister. They should be gently washed and some bicarbonate of soda lotion applied to cool them. If there are blisters, apply petroleum jelly or zinc ointment and a baby dusting powder. This rash is caused by irritation from soiled napkins or from napkins which have not been properly washed. Only the mildest soapflakes should be used for napkins. They must be thoroughly rinsed.

If the devil finds a man idle he will set him to work.

BOYS' NAMES

Abraham—Father of a multitude

Adrian—Pessimistic, hard to please

Alan—Cheerful, in harmony

Alastair—Defender of men

Albert—Nobly bright

Alexander—Helper of men

Alfred—A good counsellor

Algernon—Bewhiskered

Andrew—Manly

Aneurin—Truly golden

Angus—Pre-eminence, excellent virtue

Anthony—Strong, worthy of praise.

Archibald—Extremely bold

Arnold—Strong, eagle-like

Arthur—High-minded

Aubrey—Ruler of spirits

Austin Exalted, majestic

Barry—Straight-forward

Bartholomew—Son of the soil, a ploughman

Basil—Kingly

Benjamin—Son of the right hand (of good fortune)

Bernard—Courage of a bear

Bertram—Bright raven

Brian—Strong, sincere

Bruce—Positive, daring

Caesar—Blue-eyed

Charles—Manly

Christopher—Humorous

Clarence—Illustrious

Clement—Showing mercy

Colin—A dove, gentle

Conrad—Resolute

Cuthbert—Splendour

Cyril—Lordly

Daniel—God is my judge

David—Beloved

Denis—Love of wine and good living

Derek—People's rule

Donald—Proud, a chief

Douglas—Thoughtful

Duncan—Brown chieftain

Edgar—A spear

Edmond—Happy protection

Edward—A guard

Edwin—Happy friend

Emmanuel—God with us

Eric—Rich, powerful

Ernest—Earnest

Errol—Wandering

Eustace—Fruitful, healthy

Ferdinand—Adventurous, brave

Fergus—Strong

Francis, Frank—Dutiful son

Frederick—Peaceful ruler

Geoffrey, Godfrey—God's peace

George—A husbandman

Gerald, Gerard—Spear power

Gilbert—Bright pledge

Gregory—Watchful

Griffith—Red-haired, ruddy

Gordon—Generous

Guy—A leader

Harold—Unafraid, a warrior

Henry, Harry—Home ruler

Horace, Horatio—A punctual man

Hubert—Of a bright mind

Hugh, Hugo—Mind, thought, soul

Humphrey—Supporting peace

Isaac—Laughter

Jacob, James—The supplanter

Jeremiah—Lord lays the foundation

John, Jack—Given by God

Joseph—Fertility

Kenneth—Handsome

Lawrence—Crowned with laurel

Leopold—Prince-like

Leslie—Heroic

Lewis—Seeking fame

Lionel—Little or young, lion

Luke—Artistic

Malcolm—Kingly

Marcus, Mark, Martin—God of War

Martin—Unyielding

Matthew—Gift of the Lord

Maurice, Morris—Dark complexioned

Michael—God-like

Miles—A warrior

Great talkers are not great doers.

BOYS' NAMES (continued)—

Neil—A chief
Nicholas—Victorious
Nigel—Black, dark-skinned
Noel—Belonging to Christmas
Norman—Man of the north
Oliver—Olive tree
Oscar—A warrior
Oswald—Divine power
Owen—A lamb, or young warrior
Patrick—Noble, patriotic
Paul—Little
Percy, Percival—Companion of the chalice
Peter—Reliable
Philip—One who loves horses
Ralph, Randolf—A wolf of fame
Raymond—Wise protection
Reginald—Powerful judgment
Reuben—Behold a son
Rex—Kingly
Richard—Stern but just
Robert—Winner over all

Roderick—Famous ruler
Roger—Tall, straight
Roland, Rowland—Fame of the land
Rufus—Red-haired
Samuel—Heard of God, name of God
Sean, Shane—Irish form of JOHN
Sebastian—Venerable
Silvester—Rustic
Simeon, Simon—Obedient, one who hears
Stephen—Loyal
Terence—Tenderness
Theodore—Gift of God
Thomas—Good company
Timothy—Honoured of God
Vernon—Flourishing
Victor—Conquering
Wallace—True
Walter—Ruler
Wilfred—Resolute peace
William—Helmet of resolution

GIRLS' NAMES

Ada—Happiness
Agnes—Pure
Aileen—Light
Alice—Optimistic
Aline, Adeline—Of noble birth
Alison—Of holy fame
Amabel, Mabel—Lovable
Amelia—Toiling
Amy—Beloved woman
Angela—Angelic woman
Anita, Anne, Ann, Anna, Annabel, Annette, Annie — Grace
Annabella—Graceful, fair
April, Averil—Spring, the fourth month
Audrey—Might
Barbara—Shy
Beatrice—Blessing
Bertha—The shining one
Beryl—Precious stone
Blanche—White, purity, romance

Bridget—Strong
Carol—A Christmas child
Caroline—Feminine form of Charles
Catherine—pure
Charmian—Delight
Christine—Christian
Clara—Bright, renowned
Claudia—Lame
Constance—Firm, faithful
Diana—Goddess of light
Dinah—Judged
Dolores—Of sorrow
Doreen—Sullen
Dorothy—God's gift
Edith—Prosperous
Edna—Rich gift, pleasure
Eleanor—Light
Elizabeth—God's promise
Emerald—Precious stone
Emily—To excel
Enid—Purity
Esmé—Esteemed

Speak well of your friend, of your enemy say nothing.

GIRLS' NAMES (continued)—

Esther—Good fortune
Ethel—Noble birth
Eunice—Glorious victory
Eva, Eve—Life
Evangeline—Bearing good news
Evelyn—Giver of life
Faith, Fay—Faith
Felicity—Happiness
Flora—A flower
Florence—Blooming, fair off-
  spring
Frances—Free
Freda—Peaceful ruler
Gail—Abounding joy
Genevieve—Fair girl
Gertrude—Spear maid
Gwendoline—White browed
Hannah—Graceful
Henrietta, Harriet—Home ruler
Helen—Light
Hilary—Cheerful
Hilda—Strong
Hope—Hope
Ida—Happy
Irene—Serene, peaceful
Jane, Janet—God's grace
Jean—Loving Jane
Jennifer—Friend of peace
Joan—Gracious gift of God
Josephine—Fertility
Joyce—Sporting, merry
Judith—Praiseworthy
Julia—Changeable
June—With summer sunshine
Laura—Crowned with laurel
Lilian—Pure as a lily
Madeline, Magdalene—Penitent
Margaret—Child of light
Maria, Marie—Bitterness
Marion—Entertaining
Mary—Sympathetic
Martha—A lady
Matilda—Mighty battle maid
Millicent—Strength
Minnie—Remembrance, love

Myra—She who laments
Nancy—Grace
Naomi—Pleasant
Nelly—Light
Nina—Dissatisfied
Nora—Honourable
Odette—Of the fatherland
Olive—Bringer of peace
Pamela—Always kind
Patience—Long suffering
Patricia—Noble
Pauline—Little
Penelope—One who weaves
Philipa—One who loves horses
Phoebe—Shining
Phyllis—A green bough
Polly—A diminutive of MARY
Priscilla—Of ancient times
Prudence—Prudent
Queenie—Queen-like
Rachel—Gentle
Rebecca—A noose, or snare
Renee—Re-born
Rhoda—A rose
Rosalind—A rose
Rosemary—Unspoiled
Ruth—A friend
Sally—A princess
Sarah—Princess or Queen
Selina—The moon
Sophia—Wisdom
Stella—A star
Susan—Trusting
Sybil—Prophetess
Sylvia—Pastoral, rustic
Theodora, Dora—Gift of God
Ursula—She-bear
Vanessa—Grace of God
Valerie—Healthy
Veronica—Faithful
Virginia—A maiden
Vivien—Lively
Winifred—Peace-loving
Yvonne—Little one
Zoe—Life

Civility costs nothing but is worth much.

First + Aid

Every year thousands of housewives are injured in home accidents. Some of them are serious—falls from chairs cause the biggest number—many of them are minor accidents. To be on the safe side, every household—and particularly those with children—should have a handy first-aid box.

It need not be elaborate. Choose a fairly strong box and, of course, put it in a place where it can be easily and quickly reached. Here are some of the items you should put in it:—

Sterile dressings in sealed cartons	Burn ointment
White and pink lint	Aspirin
Oiled silk	Sal volatile
Bandages	Scissors
Cotton wool	Safety pins
Iodine	Medicine glass
	Fine tweezers

Paste your doctor's name, address, and telephone number inside the lid. And if you live in the Glasgow area it would be wise to add the emergency numbers for doctors: BEL 1212, where doctors off duty can leave their telephone number.

In cases of serious accident, the safest thing to do, after sending for the doctor, is to treat for **SHOCK.** Lay the patient comfortably, wrap him round warmly with blankets and give him hot tea or coffee —no alcohol—to sip.

Here are some of the treatments for minor accidents:—

SCRATCHES: Wipe with clean cotton wool and iodine.

CUTS: Wash and apply bandages and white lint. If dirty, put on a light, wet dressing of boric lint squeezed out in boiling water.

SCALDS and **BURNS:** If severe, treat for shock. Apply a burn dressing or bandages with burn ointment so that the air is excluded. Soaking in warm water with bicarbonate of soda is also soothing.

A clear conscience fears no accusation.

Presenting the NEW Jones!

★ **MODERNISED**
★ **STREAMLINED**
★ **BETTER THAN EVER**

... like me, you too will fall in love with the latest JONES!

FEATURES that make the latest "JONES" Gt. Britain's finest family sewing machine

★ *Simpler mechanism than any other machine, means less wear and longer life.*
★ *New self-setting needle makes wrong needle setting impossible.*
★ *Automatic Tension Release.*
★ *Sews backwards or forwards.*
★ *Stitch size adjusted at a touch.*
★ *Easy-flow presser foot rides smoothly over seams.*

Exciting news! ... Here after several years devoted to war service and the export drive is Britain's most popular sewing machine! Improved, simpler and easier than ever; spic and span in new stream-lining. Specially designed to run up that lovely new dress you've set your heart upon or to tackle *all* the family sewing. No more drudgery of hand sewing, just get a "Jones", Cash or H.P. and start sewing right away ... the right way!

It's a joy with a

Jones

Hand or electrically operated; smart new portables; Cabinet, table or treadle; all built to the standard of simplicity and reliability that has made Jones a household word for nearly 100 years.

See the latest models at—

The HUNTER MACHINE CO.

SEWING MACHINE SPECIALISTS

279 CATHEDRAL STREET - GLASGOW, C.4

— Telephone: BELL 1461 —

★ **YOUR OLD MACHINE TAKEN IN PART PAYMENT** ★

SPRAINS: Sprains are injuries of the ligaments, etc., around a joint such as the ankle or wrist; when small blood vessels are torn there is much bruising and swelling. Rest the limb and apply hot and cold compresses. Alternatively, if the injury occurs out of doors, bind the joint firmly against swelling until the patient can be rested at home.

STRAINS: Strains are caused by over exertion and are relieved by rest and hot applications. Either by hot-water bottles or fomentations.

FAINTING: If the patient is seated, bend the head forward to the knees. If on the ground, raise the feet to bring blood to the head. Loosen tight clothing. Put a cold pad on the temples until the patient is conscious. Then a cup of strong coffee or tea can be given.

BLEEDING. There are three kinds of bleeding. Bleeding from an artery, bleeding from a vein, and surface bleeding. The treatment is the same for all classes of bleeding. Place the patient in a restful position. Bleeding can usually be checked by a firm bandage.

NOSE BLEEDING: Keep the head up and tilted back. Loosen tight clothing and lay cold pads on the bridge of the nose and at the back of the neck.

POISONING: Give an emetic, e.g., one tablespoonful mustard in half-tumblerful water (but only a teaspoonful for a child).

STINGS: Remove stings and bathe place with solution of bicarbonate of soda or ammonia and water.

FOREIGN BODY IN THROAT: If possible remove with finger. Failing this, eat crusts, apple or coarse food and drink water. This failing, send for doctor.

FOREIGN BODY IN EYE: Encourage eye to water, bathe, try to remove with soft clean handkerchief. Do not rub.

FOREIGN BODY SWALLOWED: Send for doctor; eat only porridge, bread and milk, etc.

FOREIGN BODY IN EAR OR NOSE: Do not touch, but send for doctor.

FISH BONE IN THROAT: Suck half a lemon slowly to soften bone; this failing, go to the doctor.

BURNS: If the burn is extensive cover burned part with clean white rag, towel or handkerchief to exclude air and remove patient to hospital as soon as possible. Remove the clothing from the injured part unless it is sticking to the skin, in which case it must not be removed but the clothing cut round the burn. If the burn is not extensive place in warm water and, if available, add one or two teaspoonfuls of bicarbonate of soda. Just use water if the bicarbonate is not available.

More than enough is too much.

DISEASES

Almost every family, at some time or another, has close contact with an infectious disease. They are annoying, they are troublesome, but knowing a little bit about them can help prevent them from becoming serious.

Three important stages are **INCUBATION,** the period between the germs entering and the first symptoms showing; **ISOLATION,** the period when the patient is infectious and has to be kept away from others; **QUARANTINE,** the period when those who have been in contact with an infected person may develop the disease and be infectious to others. For safety, this is usually a few days longer than the incubation period.

The following are some of the most common infectious diseases with their **Incubation, Symptoms, Isolation, Quarantine, Nursing Care** and possible **Complications.**

SCARLET FEVER: Incubation, 2 to 5 days. **Symptoms:** A rapid pulse, sickness, headache, furred tongue, sore throat, fine rash usually two or three days after infection, beginning on neck and chest. The rash fades after about a week and the skin peels off. **Nursing:** Give plenty of fluids and watch the throat for any infectious discharge. **Isolation:** 6 to 8 weeks. **Quarantine:** 10 days. **Complications:** Kidney disease, rheumatism, inflammation of the ear.

MEASLES: Incubation, 10 to 18 days. **Symptoms:** A feverish and running cold with running eyes, headaches, a rise in temperature and pulse. The rash starts on forehead and behind the ears and quickly spreads. Spots are raised and blotchy and run together in patches. **Isolation:** Three weeks from appearance of rash. **Quarantine:** Three weeks. **Nursing:** Watch the eyes carefully, bathing them frequently and keeping the room shaded, and allowing very little reading. Avoid any risk of draughts or chills. **Complications:** Bronchitis, bronchial pneumonia, inflammation of ears and eyes.

GERMAN MEASLES. Incubation, 10 to 21 days. **Symptoms:** Sore throat and sometimes swelling of the neck glands. Rash begins on forehead and neck and spreads quickly. **Isolation:** 10 days from the appearance of rash. **Quarantine:** 22 days. **Nursing:** If the rash is irritating bathe with bicarbonate of soda and water. **Complications:** This is a mild disease and there are seldom any complications.

CHICKENPOX. Incubation: 2 to 3 weeks. **Symptoms:** Rise in temperature and a rash on back, shoulders, chest. They are soft, pus-filled spots. **Isolation:** Until all the scabs formed from the spots are off. **Quarantine:** 20 days. **Nursing:** Keep in bed until temperature is normal. Bathe the spots with a weak antiseptic. **Complications:** Like German measles, this is usually mild and there are seldom complications.

WHOOPING COUGH. Incubation: About 18 days. **Symptoms:** Nasal catarrh and a cough. **Isolation:** 6 weeks. **Quarantine:** 3 weeks. **Nursing:** Give fluids and do as much as possible to avoid exhaustion from coughing. **Complications:** Bronchitis and bronchial pneumonia.

MUMPS: Incubation: About 18 days. **Symptoms:** Rise in temperature and painful swelling of glands behind the ears and under the jaw. **Isolation:** One week after swelling subsides. **Quarantine:** 24 days. **Nursing:** Keep in bed until swelling is down. Light diet with a lot of liquids. Warm flannel round the neck to ease pain. **Complications:** Other glands may become infected.

In the case of all infectious diseases children require a Clearance Certificate from a doctor before they can return to school.

RINGWORM: This shows in small round patches on the scalp, chest or back. They are highly irritating and very infectious and should be treated at once by a doctor.

DIET

" I don't know why I put on weight the way that I do. It isn't as if I ate very much."

That is the heart cry of about ninety-nine per cent. of women who are overweight. It is certainly comforting to blame " glands " for the fact that the pounds mount up. But it doesn't help very much.

Better to look at it honestly and find **WHY** they mount. You may not eat a lot. But do you eat the kind of food that makes for fat—pastries, bread, potatoes, jam and sweet things?

If you are going to lose weight, you must eat the kinds of food which are low in calories and don't make weight.

It is unwise—and sometimes dangerous—to start a rigorous diet unless under doctor's orders. And in any case, most women who do this, fail to stick to it because they have attempted too much too suddenly. Or they diet strenuously for a month and then find all the weight piling on again a week or two after they have thankfully gone back to their old eating habits.

Far better to try the gradual method which brings more lasting results.

And don't be misled by some old fallacies about slimming. Lemon juice, for instance, is excellent for cleansing the system, but drinking a glass of it won't take off any weight. And a slice of bread toasted is just as weight-producing as a plain slice.

If you are the kind who fattens easily, then you have to change your whole outlook to some items. Study the Black List items which you know to be fattening (bread and all starch products, sauces, sugar, nuts, cream soups, fried foods) and tackle them.

Instead of ruthlessly cutting out all bread at once, substitute starch-reduced rolls for your breakfast bread. Cut down by, at least, half on the bread you eat later in the day and aim at cutting it out altogether. Don't eat bread at any meals where you are having potatoes. And when you do eat potatoes, have them boiled or steamed, but never fried.

If you do this sternly with all the Black List foods, you will soon begin to see results.

A word about drugs. You should never consider using these for slimming without a doctor's instruction. If you find that even gradual dieting is too big a strain on your will-power, you can now buy a three weeks' course of tablets which will help you to cut down on meals. These are **not drugs** and, in themselves, are not weight-reducing. You will still have to eat the right kind of diet foods. But these will help to take the pangs out of dieting and will supply some of the vitamins which you may be missing.

Wise people are the most modest.

Reducing Diet

If you are over-weight and if you have your doctor's permission to diet, here is a seven-day diet which will move **a** few pounds:—

	Breakfast	Lunch	Tea	Supper
SUNDAY	Orange, apple or half grapefruit Grilled rasher of bacon Tea or coffee with milk from daily ½ pint allowance small pat butter	small portion cold ham salad fruit coffee	1 cup tea 1 slice bread small pat butter	lean roast meat green vegetables 1 baked onion fresh fruit salad
MONDAY	½ grapefruit 1 grilled kipper 2 starch reduced rolls Tea or coffee	clear soup cauliflower with grated cheese but no sauce fresh fruit salad coffee	As Sunday	cold chicken or lean meat mixed salad baked apple
TUESDAY	Orange juice boiled egg starch reduced rolls small pat butter Tea or coffee	vegetable soup lunch meat celery and tomato coffee	As Sunday	baked rabbit cabbage carrot baked pear or apple
WEDNESDAY	Grilled bacon rasher and mushrooms starch reduced rolls small pat butter Tea or coffee	celery soup minced chicken or lean meat French beans apple coffee	As Sunday	2 grilled sausages mashed turnip tomatoes fresh fruit

The great and the little have need of one another.

63

REDUCTION DIET (continued)—

	Breakfast	Lunch	Tea	Supper
THURSDAY	½ grapefruit poached egg starch reduced rolls small pat butter Tea or coffee	chicken broth braised lean meat turnip, carrot apple souffle coffee	As Sunday	baked fish tomatoes stewed fruit sweetened with saccharine
FRIDAY	An apple or orange grilled bacon rasher starch reduced rolls small pat butter Tea or coffee	½ grapefruit boiled chicken carrot, turnip fruit coffee	As Sunday	grilled sole tomatoes green veget- able fresh fruit
SATURDAY	orange juice poached egg starch reduced rolls small pat butter Tea or coffee	grilled chop carrot and celery orange or apple Tea or coffee	As Sunday	meat pattie cauliflower tomatoes fresh fruit

WEIGHT CHART

For women of 25 and over. Weight with Ordinary Clothes—

Height		Small Boned		Medium Boned		Heavy Boned	
ft.	in.	st.	lbs	st.	lbs.	st.	lbs.
4	11	7	3	8	2	9	2
5	0	7	4	8	4	9	5
5	1	7	7	8	7	9	8
5	2	7	10	8	11	9	12
5	3	8	1	9	0	10	2
5	4	8	4	9	3	10	5
5	5	8	8	9	7	10	9
5	6	8	11	9	11	11	0
5	7	9	1	10	1	11	4
5	8	9	5	10	5	11	9
5	9	9	8	10	9	11	13
5	10	9	11	10	12	12	3

(Men folk should be 20 lbs. to 30 lbs. heavier.)

True lovers are shy when people are by.

THE CALORIES METHOD

Here is another way to **SLIM.** With this you need to do a little arithmetic each day.

Whether you put on weight or become slimmer depends largely on the number of calories you take. The number of calories in an article of food is the number of heat-giving units it contains. A boiled egg, for instance, is low in calories=25; a kipper=240—is very rich in calories.

Physical workers need more calories than those who spend most of their day at a desk. The average person takes 2,500 calories a day. If you want to put on weight, you can go up to 3,500. If you are reducing, try keeping to 2,000 calories a day and see the result.

When you have a craving for something sweet on a diet, turn to some of the low-calorie items instead of to biscuits or sweets. Sip a glass of tomato juice. Eat a few grapes or an apple.

Here, to help your slimming, is a list of food items with their calorie value. In each case, the amounts are average servings.

	Calories		Calories
Asparagus stalk	5	Meats, lean	150
Apples	40	Nuts, large	50
Bacon, crisp	25	Pie	300
Bread Rolls	75	Pie, custard	150
Cake	150	Potato chips, each	10
Candy bars	300	Potato baked, small	100
Celery stalk	5	Salads, light	25
Cereals, breakfast type	100	Salads, rich	100
Cheese	100	Sandwich	300
Chewing gum	1	Sausages, each	150
Water biscuits, each	25	Soups, thick	300
Butter, ½ oz.	100	Soups, thin	25
Doughnut	200	Spaghetti	200
Egg, boiled	25	Steak, medium	200
White fish	150	Vegetable, average	50
Fruit, fresh	100	Sugar, 1 spoon	25
Fruit, dried	250	Milk, 1 glass	160
Grapefruit, half	50		

They can conquer who believe they can.

Cosmetics

Few housewives have either much time or much money to spend on beauty treatments. They want to know how to make the most of themselves without attempting anything very elaborate or expensive.

It is a waste of money shopping for some magic cream that will remove spots and blemishes if you haven't first checked up on diet. The skin cannot look healthy and glowing if the blood beneath it is out of condition. Begin then, by seeing that there are enough green vegetables and raw fruit and not too much tea or coffee, too many fried foods, in your diet.

The second most basic step in skin care is **CLEANSING.** If you are lucky enough to live in a district where the water is soft and if your skin is not abnormally sensitive, soap and water should be your chief cleanser.

If your skin is older and rather sensitive, spread a good film of cleansing cream over your skin, work it lightly in, then tissue it off with soft paper tissues before washing. (You can buy deep-acting cleansers, in liquid or cream form.) This creaming takes only a minute or two extra and will leave your skin smooth and velvety—not hot or stretched—after washing.

As you get older, you have to try and keep your skin supple by replacing some of the oils which your glands no longer supply. No woman likes going to bed with any greasy cream on the skin which will be smeared on pillows and sheets. You don't have to do that to nourish your skin.

Smooth on a conditioning cream or skin food—they are now made enriched with hormones or with Vitamins A and D for older skins—immediately after cleansing. After a short time, when the skin will have absorbed most of the cream, use a tissue to remove any surplus. You get the benefit of the cream without any look of greasiness. Better still, put it on before your bath (still cleansing your face first). The steamy atmosphere will help it to soak in.

Many women find that a rich conditioning cream or oil, spread around the eyes and left on all night, causes puffiness. There are special eye creams which will nourish the very fine skin around the eyes without leaving this puffiness.

The road to hell is paved with good intentions.

MASSAGE can be very beneficial. But unless you are ready to take time to study the movements and know what you are trying to achieve it is best not to attempt it. Many good cosmetic firms supply massage charts. Another good way to learn is to spend £1 1s. having a facial treatment from an expert. This is always a good investment because you can learn from it so much about your skin and the correct use of cosmetics.

ASTRINGENTS and **SKIN TONICS** are intended to close the pores and tone the skin. They should always be patted on after cleansing and before starting make-up. That is one tip mannequins always give for a skin that stays smooth and matt, even in a hot, sticky atmosphere.

FOUNDATION. There are so many varieties of foundation on the market—light or heavy, rich or astringent, liquid or cream, tinted or natural—that there is certainly something to suit every possibly type of skin.

At one time liquid creams were inclined to be drying and were most successful on a slightly oily skin. But now they are made enriched with oils and can be used on even fine, dry skins.

If you are doubtful about the kind of cream to buy, don't be afraid to consult the salesgirl at the cosmetic counter. Very many of these girls are given training courses by famous cosmetic firms. They are well drilled in the use and purpose of the products they sell and can very often give most helpful advice.

Foundations should be used sparingly. Dab in small dots over the skin and then smooth in quickly and lightly with the fingertips.

ROUGE. Choosing the right shade is important. And here, again, the sales girl or the beauty consultant will help. There are endless tricks for using rouge to lengthen the face, widen the cheekbones and so on. But, generally speaking, this is not the kind of thing which an unskilled hand can try in a hurry. Rather put the rouge where it would naturally appear. Actress Lynne Fontaine's tip for this is to smile and then follow the rounded line of the cheek, blending the edges of the colour carefully.

If you suffer from a persistently shiny nose which not even the use of an astringent can banish, then treat it with a special anti-shine lotion before powdering.

POWDER. Again, the right shade is most important. The beauty expert in a world-famed cosmetic firm, says that most Scotswomen use too dark a shade of powder. When you have the right shade, don't dab it on. Press it on with a clean velour puff. (You can buy these rubber-filled for easy washing, quick drying). Use a small, soft, powder brush to move any surplus. This is the most lasting method of applying powder.

To hope and strive is the way to thrive.

LIPSTICK. Some women find it easier to apply lip colour with a fine lip brush. Whatever the method, shade is the most important thing. Don't attempt to change the outline but if your lower lip is very full, apply colour to the top lip only then purse the lips. You can now buy lipsticks that are non-drying and practically indelible. The beauty parlour method of applying lipstick to last is to apply it quite heavily and then to press a clean tissue between the lips.

EYE MAKE-UP is a tricky subject for the amateur. Iridescent greens and blues, properly applied, can enhance the effect of evening make-up. But it is wise to experiment once or twice before using this for any big occasion. One simple and essential part of eye make-up is to brush the eyebrows and lashes with a mascara brush to remove any powder from them. You can buy a useful browney-black mascara for mousey colouring, as well as definite brown or black. Brush your upper lashes but don't try to darken the lower ones. The effect is only hard and ageing.

Cleansing cream, skin food, astringent, foundation, powder, rouge, lipstick and mascara—these are the basis of all make-up. With the exception of cleansing cream and possibly powder—both of which should be used lavishly—they can be used quite sparingly and should last a long time. It pays to buy good cosmetics.

Just as important for daily use is a deodorant—cream or liquid— and talcum powder.

Toilet water—an inexpensive and less concentrated form of perfume —is a lovely luxury which most women refuse to give up once they have enjoyed using it. In summer time it keeps the skin wonderfully cool and fresh after a bath.

There are any number of specialised beauty preparations for particular problems.

Face masks, for instance, are not the complicated or expensive things that so many women believe them to be. They can be bought in tubes or jars (enough for a score of treatments) and using them before going out for the evening is as stimulating as a facial cocktail. Some masks are also a mild bleach and help to remove the last of a summer tan.

Those who are bothered with large pores can treat these with pore pastes. These help to stimulate the circulation and refine the skin.

For older, sagging skins there are mixtures of oils and astringents which help to firm the muscles. It is important to apply these with the correct massage movements in order to get the best out of them.

If you covet praise you do not deserve it.

You can, with a little time and trouble, give yourself a manicure as complete as a professional job.

First collect all the items you will want—lacquer remover, nail file, cuticle remover, soap and water, lacquer, cotton wool.

Wipe off the old lacquer with pads of cotton wool soaked in lacquer remover. Use a flexible emery board to round your nails and bevel the edges smoothly. If you have to do housework, you'll find it best to keep your nails fairly short. If you do break them, there is a special fixative for " repairing " broken nails so that the break is hardly visible.

Wrap an orange stick in cotton wool—a very small piece—and dip this in cuticle remover. Work it round the nails, softening the cuticle and very gently pushing it back.

Soak the finger-tips for a few minutes in warm, soapy water. Scrub very lightly with a nail brush and wipe off dead cuticle with a towel.

Apply lacquer sparingly in long, even strokes. Use an orange stick to remove any lacquer round the cuticle. It pays to apply a second coat of lacquer, but first let the under-coat dry completely.

Finish off by smoothing the hands with a softening lotion.

Even the busiest and most harrassed housewife can usually find a corner in the family luggage for the items she needs to keep her skin looking nice on holiday. If you don't take much, then you have to be sure that every item does a job.

For instance, you may find that the foundation cream you use in cold winter days is too heavy for summer. It clogs the pores and leaves your skin looking oily. Choose something lighter—a liquid, perhaps, and see that your powder shade is also lighter.

If yours is the kind of skin that burns instead of tanning, use a protective sunproof cream as your powder base. Even skins that do tan will do so more evenly and smoothly with the aid of a sun cream.

Put in some beach oil for arms, legs and body. It can be easily and safely packed now in capsules. Or you can buy it in a family-sized bottle with a spray.

Remember that it pays to buy light-weight, unbreakable bottles and jars for your powder, creams and lotions. They can be used year after year.

An ounce of discretion is worth a pound of learning.

Protect your hands

from every housework hazard

Now, at last, the toughest housework cannot spoil your hands, if you protect them first with Innoxa Barrier Creams. They safeguard your skin, prevent redness and roughness, and will not irritate the tenderest skin, nor can they affect any food you may handle.

There are two types of Innoxa Barrier Creams — Innoxa 71 for wet work, Innoxa 51 for dry. Together, they safeguard your hands, and keep them smooth and healthy, no matter how hard your work.

3/- per tube — less than 1d a day.

Obtainable from all good chemists

Innoxa

BARRIER CREAMS

INNOXA (ENGLAND) LTD. 1 EDEN ST., HAMPSTEAD RD., LONDON, N.W.

CARE OF HANDS

HANDS are the give-away for most house-wives. Hair, make-up, dress may all be perfect, but most women find it difficult to transform work-marked hands in a few minutes.

Care of the hands starts before housework is even begun. It starts with the use of a barrier cream—for wet work or dry work—which prevents dirt from going into all the small lines of the fingers in the way that is so hard to remove. Even women who protest that they can never work with gloves on can usually work easily with these " invisible " gloves.

If your hands are already badly ingrained and roughened, give them an oil bath. After washing them thoroughly in warm, soapy water, steep them leisurely in warm olive oil. When they are thoroughly soaked, massage them on a bit of old, rough, clean towelling. Repeat this once or twice more if necessary.

A nightly hand cream is essential for every housewife. Most of the good makes can be rubbed right into the skin, leaving no stickiness or greasiness. And it pays to keep a plastic bottle filled with hand lotion beside the kitchen sink.

There is one quick way to groom the hands for a special occasion. This is a new hand make-up—an opaque cream which whitens the hands and makes them look smooth and elegant.

For very chapped hands one very simple and effective remedy—glycerine and cucumber cream. This preparation should be rubbed well in whenever the hands have been in water. If your hands chap very easily it is essential to wear gloves out of doors in cool weather and you may have to wear rubber gloves when doing household washing.

CARE OF HAIR

Beautiful hair is healthy hair. If you want to get your hair into good condition you have to think not only about the things you put on it but also about your own diet and general health.

Hair texture varies as much as skin texture. Fine hair will take a perm. quicker than strong hair and needs less processing.

After checking on general health, the next care is the scalp itself. Many hairdressers now say that while constant brushing is good for the hair it can sometimes irritate the scalp. But all are agreed that the scalp itself needs friction, and that it is a good thing to press the finger-tips firmly on the scalp and move the scalp around to stimulate the circulation.

Lay a newspaper on the floor alongside your bed. Lie on your bed with your head hanging over the side and brush your hair down over the paper. This will stimulate your whole scalp.

Do as you would be done by.

Eye-strain can harm your child's sight

Her frowning painful stare of concentration is a symptom which must not be ignored. There are two sensible precautions that every parent *ought* to take: seek regular professional advice — and teach your children to use Optrex to keep their eyes relaxed, healthy and free from infection. Keep Optrex in you[r] home always — for every member [of] the family!

Oh for some Optrex

IT SOOTHES AND STRENGTHENS THE EYES

ECONOMICAL FAMILY SIZE 3/11½ ALSO AT 2/4½ AND 9[d]

If you are troubled with a flaking scalp, soak one or two cotton wool pads in hair lotion and apply these to the scalp, combing the hair into partings. Work in sections—the crown of the head, above the temples, above the ears—until you have covered the whole scalp.

If your hair is very dry, choose a shampoo that is rich in oil and use a cream conditioning treatment towards the end of the shampoo.

You will have the best results from shampooing if you have a rubber hair spray to help you rinse. A spray is one certain way of removing all the soap from the hair.

Always shampoo in two stages, using half the shampoo to move the oiliness and dirt and the other half to work up a good lather.

Hair towels must be absolutely clean. And treat the hair gently when setting it. It is at its weakest when wet.

CARE of the EYES

Most of us take our eyes for granted until they begin to bother us. The chances are that by then some damage has already been done to them.

On an average, most people use their eye muscles at almost full stretch for 15 hours a day—reading, writing and, of course, looking at T.V.!

Whatever work the eyes are doing, they ought to be given the best possible light for it. Bad light is one of the most common causes of eye-strain.

Two common eye ailments are **STYES** and **CONJUNCTIVITIS**. Styes are nothing more than little boils on the eye rim, in the sweat glands or the roots of the eyelashes. Usually they are due to local infection and the sign of a run-down condition. Eye-baths with a good eye lotion or warm fomentations with the lotion will usually clear them.

Conjunctivitis is often called " pink eye," as it very often causes the whites of the eyes to turn pink. Regular eye-bathing with an eye lotion, and rest, are the first treatment for it.

Eye bathing should start by cleansing the eyelids with clean cotton wool soaked in eye lotion to remove dust or cosmetics.

Fill an eye bath one-third full of lotion and place it against one eye with the head slightly forward. Open the eye and move the head slightly from side to side. Roll the eye round. Do the same routine with fresh lotion on the other eye.

Faults are thick where love is thin.

One of the best ways of relieving tired eyes is to lie down in a darkened room with compresses soaked in eye-lotion lying on each eye lid. But first remove all make-up and grease from round the eyes. Lie back, relaxed, in a chair with the feet up. Even 10 minutes of this can make a wonderful difference.

CARE OF TEETH: See that you visit your dentist regularly, at least once every six months. A tooth should never be extracted unless absolutely necessary. To prevent decay make sure that particles of food do not remain around the teeth after eating. It is always good to eat some firm raw fruit, such as an apple, after a meal. If your teeth fit very closely get some dental floss and use this between them every night. The teeth enjoy hard work, so it is wise to include in your diet food which requires thorough mastication. See that the teeth are thoroughly brushed behind and before, using the brush up and down more than across. And remember, do not keep a toothbrush until it is useless. To be effective a brush should be stiff.

CARE OF THE FEET: The feet have a tremendous work to do carrying much weight over long distances. Anything wrong with your feet and your whole system can be upset. The first essential is to make sure that you choose the correct shoes. They should be sufficiently long and wide to allow the feet to lie flat and straight. Make sure that you cut your nails to the shape of the toe top but never cut too short. The length of the nail should reach to the top of the toe. If you have an ingrowing toe nail lift the nail where it is pressing and insert a tiny wisp of cotton-wool soaked in peroxide and leave it in the nail to raise it. **BLISTERS:** Harden the feet by rubbing with methylated spirit. If a blister is there pierce it with a sterilised needle, drain it on clean lint, then powder with boracic. Feet, also, have too little access to the air and too little freedom from pressure of shoes. Try walking barefoot when you are certain of the cleanliness of your surroundings. Washing daily and constant change of stocking is a minimum necessity to keep your feet healthy.

Perfume is one of the more expensive items in cosmetics. But, in fact, it is not really so very expensive when you consider all the time, care and ingredients that go into the making of a really fine perfume.

There are to-day, generally speaking, three main types of perfume. **FIRST,** the concentrated type containing perhaps as many as 20 or 30 ingredients blended together.

The **SECOND** type is lighter in character and has more volume. It is made up of the same quality essences as the concentrated perfume but has a slightly more toilet-water character.

The **THIRD** is the toilet water which is meant to be used quite lavishly—as a body friction, sprinkled in cold water as a stimulating rinse, as a hair setting lotion. It is a mistake to think of toilet waters as a " poor relation " of essence perfumes. They are just as carefully blended and the ingredients are of the same high quality. They are sold in a more dilute form because the alcohol base is almost as important to the character of the toilet water as the perfume ingredients themselves.

Perfume has been used and valued from the earliest time. The Bible has many comments on perfume, incense and myrrh in particular being valued highly for their religious purposes as well as for personal uses.

In Ancient Egypt perfume was extensively used and in the tombs of the kings which have been opened up in the last twenty years beautiful specimens of the perfumer's art, from 2,000 and 3,000 B.C., have been found.

In Egypt the nobility used perfume very extravagantly and it is said of Cleopatra that the sails of her Nile barque were drenched with perfume.

In Rome, at the famous baths, masseurs rubbed in the highly-perfumed oils which kept the skin soft and fragrant.

Distilled waters were also an early perfume development and the Mediterranean countries were well able to supply the raw materials from the flowers, plants and shrubs which still grow so profusely there.

In Italy, at one time, it was the pleasant custom to make gloves from leather which had been permeated with perfumes. A famous recipient of a pair of these gloves was Queen Elizabeth who, in the 16th century, had a gift made to her by Edward Vere, the Earl of Oxford. He had brought this much-valued present back from one of his travels.

In love is no lack.

For a long time the chief sources of perfume were flowers, tree roots, etc., and animal sources.

One of these animal substances was civet and during the 16th century it was a habit of perfumers to hang up a notice with the words: "At the sign of the Civet cat," making this animal their symbol.

What is the correct way to choose a perfume? First, you must know the way to smell a fragrance. The sense of smell tires very quickly and after sniffing three or four scents, it is impossible for even the keenest nose to detect the points that matter.

Ask the salesgirl to place a drop of perfume on the wrist or back of your hand. Allow a few seconds for the alcohol to dry off and then sniff the fragrance which the warmth of your skin should bring out.

Some people turn perfumes very sweet. They should, therefore, choose a perfume with a sharp, dry note. Others, who turn perfume aromatic, should aim for sweeter, warmer tones.

CONCENTRATED PERFUMES should be used economically. A drop behind the ears, on the wrists, or a tiny wad of cotton with perfume on it tucked in the neck of a dress. Be wary about putting perfume directly on to a fabric. For one thing, you may want to use quite a different perfume the next time you are wearing that garment.

Day-time perfumes can be used less sparingly. They can be sprayed on to the skin or, perhaps, inside a handbag lining. But, remember, that all good perfumes tend to stain or may take colour from delicate fabrics.

TOILET WATERS CAN BE USED LAVISHLY. They are, of course, much less expensive than concentrated perfumes. Sprinkle a few drops of this kind of fragrance on underwear when you are ironing it.

Concentrated perfume is best bought in a reasonably small size and it should be kept, tightly stoppered, in a drawer away from the light.

Don't think that a perfume bottle is finished when it is empty. Lay it in a drawer with your underwear or, if it is a large one, hang it in your wardrobe.

A contented mind is a continual feast.

Care of cut Flowers

By JULIA CLEMENTS

The new domestic art of using flowers in the home is becoming well established as a favourite hobby with housewives everywhere. And well it should be for whether we live in town or country, on mountains or in dales, there is no time of the year when we in Scotland cannot gain access to **FLOWERS, FOLIAGE, BRANCHES** and **TWIGS** with which to make an artistic picture for home decoration.

This short guide is not intended to be an article on how to arrange flowers, but it is a guide which will help you to take care of your cut flowers, so that they last longer when placed in their favourite position in the home. It is not expected that you can remember **all** the hints after one reading, but, if you read and absorb **some** hints in the beginning and put these into practice, they soon become automatic in use. This leaves your mind free to take in a few more later on. So that if you refer to this guide again and again you will, in time, become very conversant with the needs of your plant material, which will make all the difference to the lasting qualities of your home decorations and will help you gain those extra points you need to win the prize at a flower show.

Flowers can be classified into groups, such as **FLESHY STEMMED, WOODY STEMMED, SEMI-WOODY STEMMED** and those which exude **A MILKY SUBSTANCE.** Leaves and ferns also have needs of their own, but apart from giving all plant material hours of long and deep drinking before arranging it, try to remember some of these hints. Pick **ROSES** in a partly opened bud stage. Strip off some lower leaves, split the stem and scrape off the thorns and cut notches in the outer bark of the part of the stem that will reach under water. Keep away from heat and strong sunlight. **ROSES ARE OF THE WOODY STEMMED VARIETY,** so this treatment also applies to **LILAC** (take off all the leaves and use separately), **PHILADELPHUS** (mock orange), **RIBES** (flowering currant), **RHODODENDRON** and **AZALEA,** and the ever-tantalising fluffy **MIMOSA.**

If any of these varieties flag badly, try splitting the stem ends and placing them in about two inches of boiling water, then leaving to cool. Wrap some paper round the flower heads to avoid contact with the stem, and when arranging them afterwards I usually place a teaspoonful of **SUGAR** in the ordinary **WATER.** The boiling water sounds drastic, but don't be afraid of it. I have done it and it works. All the **SEMI-WOODY VARIETY,** such as **STOCKS, CHRYSANTHEMUMS, MARIGOLDS** and **WALLFLOWERS** should have some of the outer surface of the lower ends scraped, then split. This not only allows for greater absorption of water, but helps to avoid clouding the water.

Hope is a better companion than fear.

LEWIS'S

Full Head Permanent Wave

★ **17/6**

During 97 years of Service to the Public, Lewis's have endeavoured to bring a luxury hairdressing service within the reach of the most modest incomes, and give value second-to-none in all forms of hairdressing. All the newest ideas in equipment and fittings have been installed in a Department, designed for the utmost comfort of customers.

★ *No Extras*

★ *6 Months Guarantee*

LEWIS'S · ARGYLE STREET · GLASGOW · PHONE: CEN. 9820

A certain cure for keeping the water pure is to add a tablet of **CHARCOAL.** This will absorb the bacteria or poisons in the water and so help the flowers to keep fresh. If you have added sugar to the water, don't worry—use both.

Always take off all the leaves that will come below the water line, and whether you pick or buy your flowers from the florist, always give your stems a fresh cut, before placing them in deep water. There is a theory that if you make this fresh cut under water you will avoid an air lock being formed in the stem, which has proved to be the cause of water not being able to be absorbed. I do this automatically when I am able.

Stems that exude a **MILKY SUBSTANCE,** such as **DAHLIAS, POPPIES** and **EUPHORBIAS,** can be helped if the stems are stood in boiling water or over a flame for a few seconds. This seals the cut and stops the loss of the substance.

VIOLETS, once cut, absorb moisture through their petals, so they need not reach water in an arrangement, but can be revived by plunging them heads down in water.

SWEET PEAS should not be sprayed with water, for their petals will go soggy if you do. They should be arranged lightly with grey foliage.

TULIPS love a spoonful of sugar in their water and remember, they are always better the day after they have been arranged, for they then perk up and assume a stand of their own. If you want straight Tulip stems, wrap them round in newspaper up to their heads and leave all night in a jug or tin of deep water.

Many readers ask how they can avoid **LUPINS** bending over at the top. Personally, I love to use these curves, but if you must have them straight, try cutting them **straight** across just as the lower buds are coming into flower, and don't forget to water Lupins well in the garden; dry ground is the cause of their drooping.

All **WILD FLOWERS** such as **QUEEN ANNE'S LACE, FOX-GLOVES, BLUEBELLS, ROSE BAY WILLOW HERB,** should be placed in a wrapping of wet newspaper for the journey home, then re-cut, especially the white stem ends of **BLUEBELLS,** and left overnight in deep water. This treatment will harden them and will help them to last quite a long while, but wild flowers do need hours of deep drinking before being placed in a vase. All **LEAVES** and **SPRAYS** of **FOLIAGE** should be submerged in water overnight before being used in arrangements, this applies especially to large leaves used as focal interest in a design, such as **FERNS, BEETROOT, KALE, MEGASEA,** and others of flat surface. It pays you to do this, for they become turgid and strong after such treatment.

Try preserving some **BEECH** leaves for use in winter when foliage is scarce. Put one part glycerine to two parts water in a jam jar and place some branches of Beech leaves in this solution, leaving them for three weeks. They will then have turned brown and will remain pliable and glossy all through the winter, and longer if you like to keep them.

One of these days is none of these days.

I am often asked if the use of aspirin, disinfectants or copper coins have any real effect on the length of life of cut flowers. From tests I have made, I would say, that all these things do is to help purify the water, which is better than nothing. In the meantime, my advice to all flower arrangers is to top up the vase with fresh water each day (don't change the water), drop a small **CHARCOAL TABLET** in the water, take off all leaves that will reach below water line, split woody stems, give all flowers a long drink before arranging them and leaves a deep soaking, and after completing your arrangement place in a spot away from draughts and the fumes of coal fires in winter and from heat and strong sunlight in summer. Then sit back and enjoy your lovely picture with flowers, for a longer time than previously.

Walk swiftly from temptation or it may overtake you.

IT'S A JOY...
IT'S A GOBLIN!

SAVES TIME
SAVES WORK
SAVES MONEY
SAVES WEAR
—saves my hands!

The sensational new Goblin washing machine was designed for modern homes—and the modern woman. The Goblin washer is just right—not too large for your kitchen but **big** enough for a full family wash. It washes your clothes spotlessly clean in 3-5 minutes and will take 4 lbs. of clothes at a time as well as sheets and blankets.

Complete with 10-in. adjustable and detachable wringer, casters for easy moving and beautifully finished in white enamel, the Goblin represents the finest household help a woman ever had.

Cash Price 25 GNS Plus P.T.
or on H.P. terms

DEMONSTRATIONS GLADLY ARRANGED

GOBLIN VACUUM CLEANERS

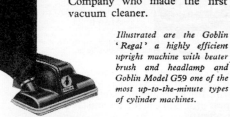

For every home there is a Goblin cleaner just suited to the household purse and need. Goblin offer the most comprehensive range of cleaners in the British Isles each backed by the 50 years' experience of the Company who made the first vacuum cleaner.

Illustrated are the Goblin 'Regal' a highly efficient upright machine with beater brush and headlamp and Goblin Model G59 one of the most up-to-the-minute types of cylinder machines.

GOBLIN *Electric Appliances*

DOMESTIC

Goblin Glasgow Branch, 13 Bath St., Glasgow. Phone Douglas 1518
Obtainable from all Electrical Dealers and Stores

MADE BY THE BRITISH VACUUM CLEANER AND ENGINEERING CO. LT

Choosing your Affinity

By CONSTANCE SHARPE

What zodiacal types suit your own character best?

It's a question well worth pondering, because in the answer lies the secret of compatability. And in searching for that answer, you will learn a whole lot more about yourself. However, to make the task easier for you, I am providing some notes on the principal affinities for each of the zodiacal signs. So all you now have to do is to look under your own birth-sign for information concerning the zodiacal types most likely to provide your affinity.

January 21   **February 19**

AQUARIUS. You have a somewhat aristocratic demeanour, and have a fondness for uncommon things and uncommon people. The ideal affinity you see is your mind's eye in all probability takes on the guise of a genius.

All things being equal, you'll get on well with some one born under **GEMINI.** For your mental and artistic urges and interests lie on the same plane; also novelty and change appeal to the pair of you.

Your second affinity is the **LIBRAN.** The traits of **AQUARIES** are in many respects similar to those of **LIBRA.** You both like bright lights and sweet music. And the Libran is as choosy of company as you are yourself.

February 20   **March 21**

PISCES. You are sympathetic, sentimental and sweet. But at the same time there are certain traits to your character which are antithetic to certain types. You will, for example, probably find yourself greatly attracted to **ARIES** types. But don't make the mistake of considering an Aries person your affinity!

Your best affinity is probably the **CANCERIAN.** You are both subject to moods, but that is the only disability. Otherwise you are a pair of sentimental, sympathetic souls, and can be the pleasantest of companions.

Your next best selection would be that of a fellow **PISCEAN!** That's a combination which should suit you well.

Think of ease but work on.

March 22   April 20

ARIES. You have a frank, direct nature, buoyant and high-spirited. But the person you see in your mind's eye as your affinity has to be something of a hero. Or, at least, something of the dash, fire and eagerness of the really spirited person.

LEO is a sign which may provide your affinity. For in Leo you will find the proud, dominating personality, superior, dignified, yet with the right amount of romance, directness and savoir-faire. The Leonian can be counted upon to quicken your interest.

A second type—and one you may think even more charming—is the **SAGITTARIAN.** Tall, chestnut hair, blue eyes, the Saggittarian has an adventurous spirit of cheery optimism, and all the romance you can take! You will find the pace remarkably swift should you link up with a Sagittarian!

April 21   May 21

TAURUS. You have a quiet, reserved nature, as well as the gift of patience. Also you have a materialistic conception of things. Which is to say you like comfort, a degree of luxury, and the best of everything. Hence you are really looking for the good provider as indispensable basis when building up your visions of your affinity.

You may find the type in **VIRGO**—tall, dark and moderately plump. For the Virgoan holds a special appeal for you. A tantalising personality, capable of arousing you from your lethargy and stimulating your expectations. Of course you probably will not enjoy the Virgoan habit of criticising, any more than the Virgoan will enjoy your own stubborn streak. But these are little things when you are gazing upon the Promised Land.

But you may prefer the hatchet-faced, ambitious **CAPRICORN** as the affinity of your dreams. For if you will give the Capricornian the necessary encouragement, the good provider will certainly materialise.

May 22   June 21

GEMINI. Basically, you are an innovator. You are for ever seeking novelties and things new. So what you really want, by way of an affinity, is a congenial companion of a calibre good enough to share your mental and artistic interests.

People swear because they know their words are worthless

The **LIBRAN** (tall, fair and handsome) will know all the answers and mentality of the Aquarian will be very similar to your own. And be short of arguments, nor will you lack conversation, if you link with Libra!

If you want a really diverting mate, chose a **SAGITTARIAN.** You won't always hit it off together. But you should have plenty of fun.

Probably your ideal affinity is an **AQUARIAN.** The ideas of Aquarius are more fixed and settled than your own. But the outlook and will prevent your mental equipment from turning rusty. You won't you will be forever swopping experiences.

June 22   July 23

CANCER. You are the domesticated type, and the kind of affinity you are seeking is the partner you can settle down with.

Your ideal may be found in **PISCES;** for the Piscean will understand your moods, and you will understand his. You'll find, too, a sentimental partner after your own heart. And once you have come together, I don't think that anything could ever separate you again.

Or you may choose a **SCORPIAN** (tall, dark and sheik-like). Scorpio is masterful and stubborn. But he is as understanding as you are fluid and adaptable. The art of persuasion can work wonders with the Scorpian!

A **GEMINIAN** may suit you best, owing to the atmosphere of change, novelty and intellectualism, which is the background music of Gemini.

On the other hand, the **AQUARIAN** is just your type. You'll find in him just the very qualities you admire the most, at the same time some one who possesses the very characteristics best adapted for keeping you in order.

July 24   August 23

LEO. You are warm-hearted and the possessor of sparkling spirits. But you do like being the boss. Therefore, to keep happy, you should choose as affinity some one who has capacity for adoring you as the leading light.

I think you should find the right degree of understanding in a **SCORPIAN.** You will, of course, be two stubborn individuals together. But you will certainly discover in each other the ideal qualities you are both seeking.

The worth of a thing is what it will bring.

You will have a good time, too, with a **SAGGITARIAN.** For your spirits will match perfectly; and in romanticism there will be a happy blend. But you must never seek to dominate the Sagittarian unnecessarily. Nothing is better calculated to produce an early break than is any attempt to shackle the freedom and independence of the Sagittarian.

You may, of course, meet your affinity in an **ARIAN.** For you have very similar spirits and should harmonise extremely well with one another (see above under ARIES).

August 24   **September 23**

VIRGO. You have the bump of curiosity enlivened by peculiarly engaging spirits. But you are remarkably choosy, as well as exceptionally critical. Consequently your selection of an affinity is not an easy matter.

You could do worse than choose a **TAUREAN.** You love to talk—and how!—and I think you will find the Taurean a remarkably patient listener. That, and the facts that he is placid, easy-going, and a good provider, may satisfy your requirements in the main.

Or you might turn to **CAPRICORN** for understanding and consideration, making a common bond of sympathy in your respective self-pitying predilections.

September 24   **October 23**

LIBRA. You know the art of pleasing, and you have many of the attributes of the coquette. You love brightness and brilliancy; but you have an eye also for the material foundation of things.

Probably your best affinity is the **LEONIAN.** And if you'll take a glance at what has been said about Leo-Sagittarius under LEO you will see the reason why.

October 24   **November 22**

SCORPIO. Magnetism, mystery, power and push. Those are the visible signs of Scorpio, the Great Lover. But you are also a born psychologist with ability to see right through the motives of people. And your deep feelings are at one and the same time your most serious weakness and your greatest strength!

Busybodies never have anything to do.

The **TAUREAN** is an excellent affinity for you since the characteristics of Taurus are the complement of your own. Of course, both of you are obstinate creatures and will have to learn the mutual lesson of give and take. But you'll get along splendidly.

The **LEONIAN** is also an excellent foil for you blending admirably on the emotional plane. But you must never forget that Leo needs attention. Should you select a Leonian, you must forever be content to remain the faithful satellite.

The **CANCERIAN** is suitable, too—provided your interests do not range outside the home. You have got to be a home-builder—that and nothing else—if you marry some one born under Cancer.

November 23   **December 22**

SAGITTARIUS. You are gay, high-spirited and disingenuous; and somehow you do seem to think that promises are like pie-crusts—made to be broken. And you have little compunction in carrying out the dual function of loving and leaving—when it suits your book. Nevertheless, you have a great power to attract, and an even greater power to charm.

ARIES suits your temperament as well as any. It's the spirit of adventure that fires your interest in the Arian. Oh yes! you'll have plenty of quarrels, but you'll find it easier to kiss and make up with an Arian than with any one else.

The **GEMINIAN** has characteristics which are complementary to your own, and you will have much in common even in the matter of your very restlessness. You will both be well attuned on the mental plane.

December 23   **January 20**

CAPRICORN. You take a serious, earnest view of life. Consequently you must mask your real feelings from the external gaze, remaining externally undemonstrative.

You get along well with the **VIRGOAN**—especially in material things and in your general attitude towards life. The Virgoan, however, is a prattler compared to yourself and this is one of the things you will have to make allowances for.

The **TAUREAN** is probably your best affinity—always provided you are not too deeply bitten with the economy bug. Share and share alike has got to be the motto here.

The **CANCERIAN** has traits which are complementary to your own, so you might possibly discover your affinity under Cancer. But you won't get very far with the Cancerian unless you are prepared to be a little demonstrative.

Law is costly, shake hands and be friends.

Birthstones

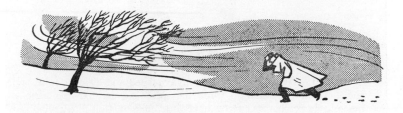

WERE YOU BORN IN JANUARY?

The **GARNET,** birthstone of the January-born has a centuries-old tradition as a precious stone.

Valued as a talisman by the ancient Egyptians, Greeks and Romans the garnet was identified as the stone of power, imbuing its wearer with the ability to command and inspire loyalty. It is also said to bestow the gift of making—and keeping—deep friendships, and to have a lucky influence on affairs of the heart, ensuring a lover's constancy. Worn as an amulet, the garnet was, in olden days, believed to preserve health and to ward off melancholy and the plague.

The fiery red garnet is most highly prized, but for the January-born the gem is equally suitable whether black, green, yellow or brown, all of which are featured in the many fashionable garnet jewel suites finding favour to-day with women born under every star.

Garnets are found in rocks which have been constantly altered by heat, chemical reaction or pressure. Hence they emanate from such countries as Burma, Siam, Ceylon, Africa, South America, the United States and India.

Their surface needs but an occasional polishing with a chamois leather in order to maintain the lustre, or may be dipped in warm, soapy water when the setting becomes dull, making sure that the stone is carefully dried with a soft cloth to prevent any dampness penetrating the setting.

He is lifeless that is faultless.

Whatever your taste in Hairdressing on the lines of your grooming, Pettigrews are Specialists in the art of emphasising, through Hairdressing, one's Personal "Chic"

Consultations freely and gladly on request

PETTIGREW & STEPHENS LTD., SAUCHIEHALL ST., GLASGOW, C.2.

TELEPHONE: DOUGLAS 2992

AMETHYST—BIRTHSTONE OF FEBRUARY.

February's birthstone, the **AMETHYST,** incomparable in colour which ranges from a delicate orchid to a glorious purple shade, is now no longer one of the most expensive of precious stones. This however is no indication of its lack of of popularity but results from a fairly recent discovery of large deposits of this lovely stone in South America.

Before these deposits were found the amethyst was both rare and expensive. The historical necklace worn by Queen Charlotte was, in fact, valued at £2,000. Catherine the Great was another admirer of amethyst, her collection being secured from the mines of the Ural Mountains—still the source of some of the finest specimens. The amethyst which adorns the Crown of England was originally taken from the ring of Edward the Confessor and is, tradition says, a prophylactic against contagious disease.

Going farther back, the amethyst was credited with a benign influence when petitions had to be made to princes, and it also held place as a " puissant preventative of hailstones and locusts." Its effect on princes perhaps explains why the signet ring of Cleopatra was an amethyst engraved with a figure of Mithras—symbol of the Divine Idea and Source of Light of Life.

A gem stone of ancient Egypt, the amethyst was also greatly favoured by the Etruscans and the Romans for intaglios. Splendid examples of amethyst sculpture include a bust of Trajan (carried off by Napoleon from the Prussian Treasury and taken to Paris); the head of Mithridates cut from a large amethyst of deepest violet and found about a century and a half ago in India; the Blacas Medusa Head and miniature reproductions of the Apollo Belvedere and the Farnese Hercules.

The name of the stone comes from the Greek and, freely translated means " not drunken." It was supposed by the ancients to prevent intoxication when worn about the person, while another theory held that wine taken from an amethyst cup had little ill effect. To complete its romantic history, mention must be made that it is the distinctive stone of Bishops and also, incongruously, that of Bacchus.

More materially, the amethyst is the most valuable of the quartz stones. Chemical analysis reveals manganese, titanium and iron in its composition, and while its colour has been attributed to the presence of manganese, a study of the absorption-spectra suggests that iron in a collodial form may really be responsible.

Observation is the best teacher.

In the middle of the nineteenth century it was fashionable to set small stones into larger ones and small diamond stars would be set in the large amethysts of a necklace, or tiny flowers into ear-rings. The return to favour of jewellery of Victorian design has focussed attention again on the amethyst and, although fashion, and the sentimental regard of those whose birthstone it is are aids to its popularity, its own extraordinary beauty will always make it a treasured feminine adornment.

BIRTHSTONE OF MARCH.

The **AQUAMARINE,** with its Latin name meaning " sea water," is perhaps the most appropriately-named of all gem stones, for it has also been described as " having come direct from some mermaid's treasure-house in the depths of a summer sea."

A species of the mineral **BERYL,** the aquamarine is closely related to the emerald, though not so rare. It is especially noted for its ability to harmonise with any colour and for the fact that it does not lose any of its splendour in artificial light.

This lovely birthstone of March (incidentally, one of the favourite jewels of Queen Elizabeth, the Queen Mother) was in olden days worn as an amulet and known as the " stone of safety." It was also said to bring solace and comfort in times of stress and trouble and has, throughout the centuries, been worn to ensure happiness in marriage.

The unusual colouring of the aquamarine is said to be due to the presence of ferric oxide in an otherwise pure and colourless beryl. The stone is found in the Urals of Russia in prolific quantities; in many other parts of the world as widely separated as Madagascar and California, and in Brazil from whence many of the largest specimens have originated. It has also been found in India, where at one time it was fashionable to have it cut into long, cylindrical beads and strung on elephant hair.

The Romans chose the aquamarine as the most suitable stone for faceting and they also wore it in the form of ear-drops and in unengraved rings. Later, it was a favourite engraving stone of European Renaissance artists.

In pre-Victorian times the greenish variety of this gem stone was chiefly worn, but in modern times the preference is for the pure, light-blue variety which Rosetti so aptly describes as " rainbow lured through a misty pall, like the middle light of a waterfall."

Those born in March are specially favoured in having this beautiful gem as their birthstone. Not only is its translucent colouring flattering to both brunette and blonde alike, but because of its legendary power of "increasing and preserving married love" it is a popular choice for engagement rings, particularly for those whose birthstone it also happens to be.

WERE YOU BORN IN APRIL?

Acclaimed over a thousand years ago as "the most valuable thing on earth," the **DIAMOND** still holds pride of place among all precious gems. Birthstone of the April-born, its dazzling history is full of romance and glamour, and its influence over human affairs has always been thought to be more powerful than that of any other stone.

The name of this matchless gem is derived from "Adamas," meaning "the Indomitable"—probably because the diamond is the hardest known substance, and in ancient times was valued more for its physical and mystic qualities than for its beauty. The symbol of purity and innocence, it has a legendary power of protecting its wearers from evil, especially when worn on the left side of the person. In India tiny diamonds are sprinkled over the baby's head during the naming ceremony to endow the child with purity and virtue.

Many famous people have believed in the diamond's mystic powers. Queen Elizabeth wore one as a guard against infection, and Napoleon had the magnificent Regent diamond set as a talisman in his sword hilt. According to the Ancients, if a diamond was to bring luck it had to be "given freely, never sold by its owner, never lent, never coveted and never taken by fraud or force," while to lose a diamond was supposed to be an omen of even further misfortune.

To-day the diamond reigns supreme in modern jewellery. Improved methods of cutting and setting have given it a greater beauty and brilliance than ever before. Those who wish to wear their April birthstone have a better than ever choice of designs from which to select their own distinctive diamond.

As with all precious stones of a hard surface, the diamond may be immersed in warm water, provided care is taken not to loosen the setting.

Don't cry over spilt milk.

WERE YOU BORN IN MAY?

The **EMERALD,** birthstone of the May-born, is as much prized to-day as it was 3,000 years ago when, because of its rare beauty, the ancient Egyptians considered it a stone of the Gods.

In those bygone days sacred images had flashing emerald eyes. Later, the Mohammedans believed that a rough emerald inscribed with a verse of the Koran was a talisman of immortality. They also regarded the gem as a symbol of constancy and true affection—a belief which still exists and may account for the popularity of emeralds as engagement rings.

The finest emeralds are found in Siberia, India and Mexico. The Incas of Peru possessed an emerald the size of an ostrich egg which was supposed to be inhabited by Esmeralda, chief goddess of the country. For this reason the Peruvians regarded their emerald mines as sacred.

A highly polished emerald was once believed to have the power of restoring failing eyesight, and Nero, watching gladiators in the arena, used an emerald to lengthen his vision.

The emerald is probably best-known as the talisman of sailors. Suspended from the neck so that the gem lies against the breast, an uncut emerald is supposed to preserve fishermen and other seafarers from perils.

The fashionable woman also wears emeralds round her neck, though these are most beautifully cut and mounted in precious metal, and usually matched by emerald ear-rings, bracelet and ring.

WERE YOU BORN IN JUNE?

The perennially fashionable **PEARL** is the birthstone of those born in June. Romance and tradition have surrounded this gleaming gem for thousands of years.

In the East the pearl is still the most popular talisman, and is thought to give profound wisdom to the wearer. They are also thought to preserve the purity of those who wear them.

Life lies not in living but in liking.

The Romans set high value on pearls, consecrating them to Isis, and believing that by wearing the gem they would obtain the goddess's favours. In the Middle Ages pearls were worn for the luck they could bring and men carried their pearls with them into battle.

The pearl is the " constant " gem, supposedly capable of endearing the wearer to friends and enemies alike, and of protecting the wearer from all harm. In olden days divers wore a pearl as an amulet to protect them from sharks.

So strong are the traditions associated with the pearl that members of old families leave instructions in their wills that the family pearls must never pass into other hands, in case the hereditary fortunes be adversely affected.

Beautiful women throughout the ages, including Cleopatra, whose pearls were legendary, have worn fine pearls.

Pearls should never become immersed in water. Their natural oil is maintained by constant wearing next to the skin, and care should be taken that they are not placed near other harder stones which might scratch their surface.

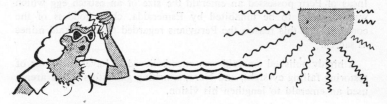

WERE YOU BORN IN JULY?

The **RUBY,** birthstone of the July-born, has for centuries been credited with ensuring marital bliss and success in matters of the heart. Tradition also has it that those who wear the ruby are generous and thoughtful to those in less fortunate circumstances.

Besides attracting love and devotion, this blood-red gem has been attributed with the power of rekindling love that has waned. Many women born in July have doubly ensured themselves of obtaining the ruby's powers by choosing the gem for their engagement ring as well as for their birthstone.

It was believed by the ancients that the ruby enabled the wearer to to overcome temptation, and for thousands of years the gem has been associated with bodily, as well as mental, health. In the Middle Ages the ruby was endowed with many curious powers, including the capacity to bring relief in pain, to protect the wearer against drowning and to cure rheumatism.

While moderns may not share ancient beliefs in the ruby's powers, the gem's beauty is, at least, as much appreciated to-day as it has ever been. Evidence of this may be seen in the many magnificent pieces of modern jewellery which feature the ruby.

Rubies are found in Burma, Siam and Ceylon.

A wise man changes his mind a fool never will.

WERE YOU BORN IN AUGUST?

Those born in August are particularly fortunate in having two birthstones from which to choose, the choice probably depending upon colour preference—the deep bottle-green **PERIDOT** or the rich red-brown **SARDONYX**.

When Job praised the value of wisdom and said, " The Topaz of Ethiopia shall not equal it," he referred to what we know to-day as the peridot.

Among the virtues claimed by the ancients for this gem was its power to dispel physical and mental timidity—the " inferiority complex " of to-day.

Considered to be a good omen in marriage, the peridot is said to bring gladness, serenity and faithfulness.

The " evening emerald " has been one description of the peridot, which may be pronounced in the French way to rhyme with " go," or Anglicized to rhyme with " got."

Great powers of endurance and courage were thought to be the virtues conferred upon the wearer of the sardonyx in bygone times.

Not the least of this gem's reputed virtues is the ability of its wearer to become much-sought after.

The hard, smooth surface of the sardonyx is particularly suitable for carving. Large stones often have as many as three or four layers, permitting designs to be cut in high relief and set in intaglio fashion. The figure of Mars or Hercules was often carved on the sardonyx by the ancient Romans, who believed that the value of the stone was increased if suitably engraved.

The world's largest sardonyx, engraved with a scene of a triumphant Bacchus, is now among the Vatican treasures. It is in cameo form and measures 18 inches by 12 inches—nearly a dozen times the size of the usual sardonyx cameo.

Muddle at home makes the husband roam.

WERE YOU BORN IN SEPTEMBER?

If you were born in September you can claim as your birthstone a gem which was one of the first stones which men held to be precious —the **SAPPHIRE**. There are many Biblical references to this lovely " heaven-hued " gem; Moses' rod was set with sapphires, and so was the sealstone of King Solomon's ring. Later on, in the 4th century, St. Jerome declared that the sapphire's inherent virtue " procures favours with princes, pacifies enemies, frees from enchantment and maintains freedom from captivity," while in the 12th century Pope Innocent III decreed that an engraved sapphire, because of its purity and light should be used for Bishops' rings.

Because of its association with truth and virtue, men in the Middle Ages wore the sapphire as a protection against the Black Arts, while should any treacherous person wear the stone it was supposed to become pale and lack lustre.

Above all, the sapphire, which symbolises constancy, is the traditional lovers' stone. Two rough sapphires were given by the Emperor Charlemagne to his wife as a love-talisman, and when she died the stones, strung round her neck, were buried with her.

To-day many modern couples are choosing engagement rings set with sapphires, as solitaires, combined with diamonds or other stones, or set into an eternity ring. The rich midnight blue sapphire is perhaps most sought after, but all shades are in demand; while the September-born who prefer another colour can choose their birth-stone in pink, mauve, violet, green, yellow, golden brown or white. Many fashionable jewel-pieces feature sapphires as, for instance, a magnificent dress clip set with massed sapphires cut en cabochon, while, in line with the vogue for more colourful jewel designs, sapphires of different hues are often used together, a combination of blue and yellow stones looking particularly attractive.

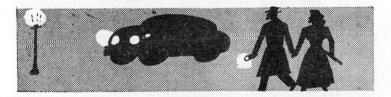

WERE YOU BORN IN OCTOBER?

Fire-flashing **OPAL** is the birth-stone of the October-born. This highly attractive gem has been described as having " the living fire of the ruby, the glorious purple of the amethyst and the sea-green of the emerald."

He that doth lend doth lose his friend.

No other gem has been the centre of so much controversy and superstition as the opal, though few people to-day share the unfounded Victorian belief that opals are unlucky.

The ancients had no fear of the opal. On the contrary, they believed it bestowed every possible benefit on the wearer. It was called the " gem of hope," and was supposed to bring romance into the lives of all who wore it. Lasting love and affection were believed to remain wherever the opal was.

In the East it was thought that the opal had the power to improve eyesight and the memory. To effect these benefits, the " holy men " touched the brows of their patients with opals.

No two opals are alike in appearance. Some are as pale as milk, with shading of pink and green. " Rainbow " opals gleam with almost every colour, while " fire " opals have an orange-pink radiance. The rare black opal has red, green and purple tones predominating.

The wide range of colour embodied in opals undoubtedly accounts for their present popularity, since colour is the keynote of to-day's jewel fashions. In addition to the very attractive rings which have an opal as the centre stone surrounded by small pearls, opals are being seen with increasing frequency in the form of necklaces, bracelets and ear-rings, usually combined with another brilliant gem such as garnet, sapphire or emerald.

WERE YOU BORN IN NOVEMBER?

There is an old rhyme which runs:

" Firm friendship is November's and she bears
True love beneath the topaz that she wears."

The **TOPAZ**, birthstone of those born in November, was well known to the ancients. A topaz is among the nine precious stones in the Nan Ratan, the most important and sacred ornament in the Burmese regalia. Pliny, who called the topaz the " Stone of Strength," stated that the gem's name was derived from the island of Topazon in the Red Sea.

The Roman Emperor Hadrian was among those who believed in the powers of the topaz. He possessed a ring set with a topaz which bore an inscription prophesying good luck to the wearer. The ancients believed that the powers of the topaz increased as the moon waxed and decreased as it waned.

When out of sorts give nature a chance.

In the Middle Ages a topaz set in gold and hung about the neck was believed to give protection against enchantment. Among its other supposed virtues were its ability to cure insomnia and illnesses of the throat and lungs.

In more recent times the topaz has been credited with the power to ensure a lover's fidelity and the loyalty of friends.

The colours of topaz are many, including blue, light green, sherry, rose and, of course, yellow. The Empress of Austria possessed a famous pink topaz, which was oval in shape and over one one-quarter inches in length. This magnificent gem has now been re-cut by a London jeweller and set in a ring.

Gold is still the most popular setting for the topaz, as can be seen in the highly fashionable " bib " necklaces with matching " chandelier " ear-rings and bracelets which radiate the unsurpassable glow achieved by the combination of the golden topaz with golden metal.

WERE YOU BORN IN DECEMBER?

The **TURQUOISE**, birthstone of the December-born, is so called because, in ancient times, it was brought through Turkey on its way to Europe from Persia.

This lovely blue-green gem, which is enormously popular to-day, and figures prominently in a variety of jewel creations, has for centuries been considered the stone for lovers, since it is said to dispel the jealousy of rivals and to ensure the fidelity of those in love. As the poet wrote:

> " No other gem than turquoise on her breast
> Can to the loving, doubting heart bring rest."

The Turks looked upon this gem as the horseman's talisman. It is supposed to protect both the rider and his mount, and to guard the rider against fatigue on long journeys.

The oldest dated piece of jewellery is said to be an Egyptian bracelet set with turquoise, which probably came from the ancient mines of the Sinai Peninsula. The finest turquoise has always come from Persia, which undoubtedly accounts for it being regarded by the Persians as their national gem.

More haste less speed.

Going on Holiday

Shutting up a house is a tiresome job which can be made easier if you keep a list like the following beside you and tick off the points as you attend to them.

1. Tell the **POLICE**. Give them the dates you will be away and tell them where you are leaving your keys.

2. Turn off **WATER, GAS, ELECTRICITY**. And if you have any fears about burst pipes, empty the tank.

3. Stop deliveries of **MILK, PAPERS,** etc. And remember to give a date for re-starting.

4. Check that there is no **FOOD** in cupboards other than the tinned or packet variety that will be useful when you return. Leave empty bread bins and tins open to air.

5. Secure all **WINDOW FASTENINGS** and **LOCKS**.

6. Stuff some newspapers up the **CHIMNEY** as a precaution against a blow-down of soot. Or make a more secure job by pasting brown paper across the fireplace opening.

7. Clean out all flower **VASES**.

8. Having done all these things, **GO AWAY WITH AN EASY MIND.**

None so blind as those who won't see.

Anniversaries

Most people know that a silver wedding falls on the 25th anniversary and a golden wedding on the 50th. But do you know all the other anniversaries?

Anniversary	Wedding
First	Cotton
Second	Paper
Third	Leather
Fifth	Wooden
Seventh	Woollen
Tenth	Tin
Twelfth	Silk
Fifteenth	Crystal
Twentieth	China
Twenty-fifth	Silver
Thirtieth	Pearl
Fortieth	Ruby
Fiftieth	Golden
Sixtieth	Diamond

Self praise is no recommendation.

With a good stock as a basis you can very soon produce an excellent soup. For stock you should boil meat bones with bacon rind and vegetables and add a bouquet garni (peppercorns, 1 blade mace, 1 bay leaf, parsley stem, 2 cloves, strip of lemon rind) tied in muslin for flavouring.

MOCK KIDNEY SOUP

Half-pound liver, pieces of carrot, turnip, 2 small onions, 1 oz. cooking fat, 2 pints stock, seasoning, flour, pinch of sugar.

Heat the sugar in a pan until caramelled. Melt the fat and dry the thinly sliced onions. When these are deep brown, add carrot and turnip and fry lightly. Wash and clean the liver, cut in pieces, dry and toss in flour.

Draw the vegetables to the side of the pan and fry the liver, using more fat if necessary. Pour in stock and seasoning and simmer two hours. Strain. Dice the liver. Measure the soup and allow 1 tablespoon flour per pint. Blend measured flour with cold water, return to the pan with soup and diced liver. Stir until boiling. Season to taste.

CHICKEN BROTH

Joints of chicken, 1 onion, 2 ozs. rice, 1 to 2 leeks, chopped parsley, 4 pints stock.

Season the chicken joints lightly with salt and pepper. Put in a pan with sliced onion, add stock, and simmer gently for three hours. Strain and return stock to the pan Add well-washed rice and chopped leek. Cook about 30 minutes, until rice is tender. Season to taste and add chicken flesh cut small. Stir in some chopped parsley and serve.

An hour in the morning is worth two in the evening.

SOUP NOTES

SOUP NOTES

Fish is very good for us. And, no doubt, many of us would eat more if it were cooked with greater variety. For instance, fish with no great individual flavour is improved if cooked and served with cheese.

HADDOCK AU GRATIN

Three gills Bechamel sauce, ½ oz. margarine, 2 ozs grated cheese, 8 to 12 ozs. cooked haddock, seasoning.

Simmer the sauce 10 minutes. Beat in margarine in small pieces just before using. Mix the flaked fish with the sauce, season well and stir in most of the cheese. Pour into a shallow casserole or fireproof dish. Sprinkle remaining cheese over and brown in the oven. Serve very hot.

BECHAMEL SAUCE

Three gills milk, small pieces carrot, turnip and onion, 6 peppercorns, small piece of mace, bay leaf, parsley stem, 1 oz. cooking fat, 1½ ozs. flour, pepper, lemon juice, salt vinegar.

Simmer milk and flavourings 15 minutes in a covered pan. Strain. Melt the fat, add flour, and stir slowly in milk until boiling. Season to taste.

SCALLOPED FISH

Three gills Bechamel sauce, 8 to 12 ozs. cooked white fish, breadcrumbs, 1 lb sieved potatoes, 1 oz. margarine, seasoning, a little milk.

Melt the margarine and add, with seasoning and a little milk, to the sieved potato. Make a deep border of potato round a shallow fireproof dish—use two spoons for this. Spread a layer of flaked fish in the middle of the dish. Cover well with sauce then continue with another layer of fish followed by sauce. Sprinkle browned crumbs on thickly and heat through in the oven. Serve with sliced lemon.

Nothing is cheap if you don't need it.

FISH NOTES

FISH NOTES

(1) If you have any cooking Kippers over and have any left over immediately cool it as quickly as possible before reheating, let no smoke it next time.

(2) We have had some customers who bought meat and say on Friday or Saturday, bringing it back home on the Monday, and naively explain that the meat is too lean they had cooked it. This is merely that when the meat go back they should have rinsed it all over with dry salt, and left it in a cool place, till required for cooking, or should have thoroughly cooked it.

(3) We have had customers who kept Kilns simmering for hours even after they had been turned, and then people in the sun. There is another instance where lack of quick cooking, as also the water had...

(4) All Fish are made without ventilation hole at the top, else the reason for this again, if quick cooking otherwise the fat could be bad in a few hours.

(5) When cooking Pickled Beef, don't keep boiling it, bring it to the boil from cold and reduce your heat to 200 degrees F. or less. This applies also to cooking Hams and Meats.

(6) Pickled Tongues, Half Tongue for an hour hard, take out of pot and plunge into cold water and in a couple more shelves of them equally in pot and simmer for no less than one hour, or even an hour from that, value on a table. The tongue may not be as tender as beef but tender and eaten cold, will be surrounded by a clear hard jelly, it becomes more like Bacon Joint than the meat it was cooked, in that also there is reason enough. Pork pickled and Ox Tongues are two things great to serve out cold.

(7) Sausages Should be cooked by shaking cold pan, gradually bringing heat up to a good cooking point and cook instead with a done.

(8) If you are missing stock from Meats, it simply matter how many hours you boil them, but keep them simmering, till you reach the boiling point, else lose flavour in cooking.

If any Householder has any DIFFICULTY Mr. GRANT will be delighted to answer them.

* H

JAMES GRANT

GLASGOW'S FOREMOST FLESHER

Offers the following tips :

(1) If you have been cooking Mince or Stew and have some left over, thoroughly cool it as quickly as possible before replacing lid, otherwise it won't keep.

(2) We have had some customers who bought meat on, say, a Friday or Saturday, bringing it back rotten on the Monday, and naively explaining that owing to the heat they half-cooked it. This is exactly what made the meat go bad; they should have rubbed it all over with dry salt, and left it in a cool place, till required for cooking, or should have thoroughly cooked it.

(3) We have had customers who kept Mince simmering for hours (even after they had used some) and then merely turning out the gas. This is another instance where lack of quick cooling can send the Mince bad.

(4) All Pies are made with a ventilation hole on the top crust, the reason for this again is quick cooling, otherwise the pie could be bad in a few hours.

(5) When cooking Pickled Beef—**don't keep boiling it**—bring it to the boil from cold and reduce your heat to 200 degrees F., or less. This applies also to cooking Stews and Mince.

(6) **Pickled Tongues.**—Boil tongue for an hour hard, take out of pot and plunge into cold water to take skin off, then replace in pot and simmer for no less than five hours, or even six hours, in as little water as possible. The tongue can now be put in basin or bowl for pressing and, when cold, will be surrounded by a delightful jelly. If you don't want to press the tongue, leave it in the water it was cooked in, but see that it cools quickly. Pickled Beef and Ox Tongues are two things most housewives undercook.

(7) Sausages should be cooked from a cold pan, gradually bringing heat up; a good sausage does not need pricked with a fork.

(8) If you are making stock from Bones, it doesn't matter how many hours you boil them, but keep them simmering till you need the stock—your stock loses flavour on cooling.

★ **If any Housewife has any QUERIES, Mr. GRANT will be delighted to answer them.**

For

QUALITY MEAT, MUTTON, PORK...

Shop at

JAMES GRANT

88 STOCKWELL STREET, GLASGOW, C.1

86 SALTMARKET

183 COWCADDENS STREET

1068 ARGYLE STREET

182 LONDON ROAD
144 NEW CITY ROAD
252 DUMBARTON ROAD
311 DUMBARTON ROAD

40 GLASGOW ROAD, CLYDEBANK
2 CHURCH PLACE, OLD KILPATRICK

Cooking a large cut of meat is never a very difficult business. It is when the housewife has to spin out a small quantity or make left-overs interesting that she has to use her imagination.

RABBIT AND HAM ROLL

One **RABBIT**, 6 ozs. raw **BACON**, 6 ozs. **BREADCRUMBS**, 2 raw **EGGS**, 1 to 2 **HARD-BOILED EGGS**, 1 small finely-chopped **ONION**, 1 teaspoon grated **LEMON RIND**, 2 teaspoons chopped **PARSLEY**, pinch of **HERBS**, 1 gill **STOCK, SALT, PEPPER.**

Joint rabbit, soak in salted water for 30 minutes. Dry and take flesh from bones. Cut this in small pieces and mince with the ham. Mix together everything except the hard-boiled eggs. Pound with the end of a rolling pin. Turn on to a floured board and roll into a square. Spread all over with slices of hard-boiled egg. Roll up carefully into a roly poly. Scald and flour a strong cloth and tie the roll tightly in this.

Plunge into a pan with boiling water to cover. Boil gently two hours with the bones, replenishing when necessary with boiling water. Take the roll from the cloth and tie up tightly in a dry cloth. Press overnight between two flat plates with a weight on top. Remove the cloth, brush with glaze and serve.

GLAZE

One teaspoon **MEAT** or **VEGETABLE EXTRACT**, ½ gill **STOCK**, ¼ oz. **GELATIN.** Melt together over heat. Cool slightly before using.

Health is better than wealth.

MEAT NOTES

MEAT NOTES

Some hours we should find for the pleasure of the mind

PRIMULA CHEESE *FOR TEA*

FOR HEALTH and ENERGY

Primula Cheese Spread is a family favourite all over the world.

It combines delicacy, mild flavour and a cream-like consistency.

Use it as a spread, it is lovely with fruit and a perfect flavouring for soups and other dishes. It adds cleverness to simple cookery.

PRIMULA

The Crispest

CRISPBREAD

Made from selected unadulterated whole Rye. A perfect health food. Take it with every meal, it is non-fattening, and very nourishing. A popular slimming diet.

CHILDREN LOVE PRIMULA CRISPBREAD SPREAD WITH PRIMULA CHEESE.

STOCKED BY ALL GOOD GROCERS

KAVLI PRODUCTS FOR PURITY AND GOOD HEALTH

PUDDINGS and DESSERTS

Many housewives who are not over-fond of cooking admit that they quite enjoy making puddings and desserts. There is so much scope for variety. Here are some simple ideas for family dinners.

BAKED LEMON CURD PUDDING

One pint **MILK**, 2 ozs. **SEMOLINA**, 1 oz. **MARGARINE**, 1 oz. **SUGAR**, 2 **EGGS**, rind of half a **LEMON**, lemon **CURD**.

Heat the lemon rind and milk and sprinkle in the semolina. Boil five minutes then add margarine. When slightly cooled, add beaten eggs and sugar.

Turn into a greased pie-dish and bake until firm. Spread with lemon curd. Whisk the whites stiffly adding some castor sugar, and pile on top of the curd. Return to a cool oven for about 15 minutes to make firm and brown on top.

CHERRY TART

Two and a half ounces short **CRUST PASTRY**, 1 lb. **CHERRIES**, 1 gill **WATER**, 4 ozs. **SUGAR**, squeeze of **LEMON JUICE**, 1 teaspoon **ARROWROOT, COCHINEAL**, ¼ oz. **MARGARINE**, some whipped " **CREAM."**

Line a flan case with the pastry. Fill with beans or crusts and bake 20 minutes in a fairly hot oven—Regulo E. Remove the crusts and return the case to the oven to dry off. Cool on a tray.

Make a syrup of water, sugar and lemon juice. Boil for 2 minutes. Stone the cherries and cook very slowly until tender but not broken down. Strain the fruit. Return the juice to the pan with arrowroot blended with cold water.

Stir until boiling. Add colouring and margarine. Fill up the case with cherries. Pour over the cooled syrup. Serve when quite cold, decorated with whirls of cream.

FRUIT DUMPLING

Four ounces **FLOUR**, 3 ozs. **BREADCRUMBS**, ¼ teaspoon **BICARBONATE OF SODA**, 3 ozs. chopped **SUET**, 3 ozs. **BROWN SUGAR**, 2 ozs. **CURRANTS**, 4 ozs. chopped **RAISINS** (or dates), ½ **ORANGE**, ½ grated **CARROT**, ½ teaspoon each ground **GINGER, CINNAMON** and Mixed **SPICE**, a little **MILK**.

Marry in haste and repent in leisure.

Wash and dry the fruit, squeeze the orange and grate the rind. Mix all the dry ingredients and add the carrot, orange rind and juice and enough milk to make a fairly soft dough. Turn into a scalded and floured cloth. Tie tightly with string, leaving room for the dumpling to rise.

Sit it on a plate in a pan of boiling water. With the lid on, boil steadily 2 to 3 hours, replenishing with boiling water when necessary. Turn on to a hot ashet, carefully removing the cloth and serve the dumpling at once.

NOTES

He is unfortunate who cannot bear misfortune.

PUDDING and DESSERT NOTES

Second thoughts are often best.

CAKES and BAKING

With sugar unrationed and white flour back again there is some incentive for the housewife to take a pride in her baking. Here are some hints on cake-making and one or two recipes.

1. **WASH** and dry all fruit before using. Damp fruit tends to sink.
2. **GLYCERINE** added to margarine helps to keep the cake moist —1 teaspoon glycerine for quantities up to 2 lbs. margarine.
3. Break **EGGS** separately into a cup before mixing.
4. **BROWN SUGAR** can be used instead of castor for dark cakes.
5. Use a **WOODEN SPOON** or your hand, for mixing.
6. Line the tin, bottom and sides, with two or three layers of **GREASEPROOF PAPER.** Greasing the tin is not necessary.
7. Heat the oven to required setting before putting the cake in. This usually takes 20 minutes. Put the shelf about half-way up the oven.
8. Don't open the door for, at least, **30 MINUTES** after putting in a cake—and then only if you must. Test for readiness with a heated knitting needle.

SULTANA CAKE

Eight ounces **MARGARINE**, 8 ozs. Castor **SUGAR**, 12 ozs. **FLOUR**, 12 ozs. **SULTANAS**, ½ teaspoon **BAKING POWDER**, 1 teaspoon **GLYCERINE**, ½ teaspoon **VANILLA**, 4 to 6 **EGGS**.

Wash and dry the fruit. Toss in a little flour. Beat 4 eggs with glycerine until frothy. Sift the flour and baking powder. Cream the margarine and sugar. Add eggs and flour alternately, using more eggs if necessary. The mixture must not be too stiff. Stir in fruit and flavouring and bake in prepared tins 20 minutes at Regulo E, one hour at Regulo D, and about one more hour at Regulo C.

NAPLES CAKES

Four ounces **MARGARINE**, 4 ozs. **FLOUR**, 1 **YOLK**, 2 ozs. castor **SUGAR**, 2 ozs. ground **ALMONDS**, grated rind of **ORANGE** or **LEMON JAM, CHOCOLATE BUTTER**, ½ oz. blanched **ALMONDS** shredded and baked golden brown.

Rub the fat into the flour and add the dry ingredients. Mix well and bind stiffly with egg. Knead until smooth. Roll out ⅓-inch thick and cut in 2-inch diameter rounds. Bake at Regulo E until light brown. Cool and sandwich with chocolate butter. Sprinkle with baked almonds.

Every ass loves to hear himself bray.

The Best Paint you can buy –

YOU can't buy a better Gloss Paint than "Superlative." It is well known as "The Best Gloss Paint in the World." And this is true. It is true that homes protected with "Superlative" are well protected for years longer than they could be with any ordinary paint. "Superlative" Paint is so tough, so wonderfully durable, that it is chosen above all others in countries all over the world to protect great and important bridges and to beautify public buildings. The lovely, mirror-like finish is easy to wash down too, so "Superlative" saves cleaning time and labour; forty delightful colours; packed in ½ pint to 1 gallon tins. From all good paint shops.

– it's "Superlative"

Ask your paint shop for details of other fine paints by the makers of "Superlative."

Superlative GLOSS PAINT

BRITISH PAINTS LIMITED

57-59 CORNWALL STREET, KINNING PARK, GLASGOW.

CHOCOLATE BUTTER

One ounce **MARGARINE**, 2 ozs. **ICING SUGAR**, ½ oz. **CHOCO-LATE, VANILLA.**

Grate the chocolate and melt over hot water. Add to creamed margarine and sugar. Flavour.

FRUIT BUNS

Eight ounces **FLOUR**, 2 ozs. **MARGARINE**, 2 ozs. castor **SUGAR**, 2 ozs. **CURRANTS**, 1 oz. chopped **GLACE CHERRIES**, 2 teaspoons **BAKING POWDER**, 1 teaspoon mixed **SPICE**, 1 **EGG**, about 1 gill **MILK.**

Rub the margarine into the flour and add the dry ingredients. Mix with beaten egg and milk. Using two forks, form into rough little heaps on a greased baking sheet. Sprinkle with sugar and bake quickly, about 15 minutes, in a hot oven.

ICED BISCUITS

Eight ounces **FLOUR**, 4 ozs. **MARGARINE**, 4 ozs. **CASTOR SUGAR**, 1 **EGG**, ¼ teaspoon **BAKING POWDER.**

Cream the margarine and sugar. Gradually add flour, baking powder and egg, working smoothly together. Set aside in a cool place to become stiff. Roll out thinly on a floured board and cut into small biscuits. Put a teaspoon of water icing on each and decorate with small pieces of cherry. Make the icing by blending 1 tablespoon of boiling water and 4 ozs. sieved icing sugar, flavouring and colouring as liked. Bake until crisp at Regulo E.

NOTES

Who never tries cannot win the prize.

BRITISH WEIGHTS AND MEASURES

AND THEIR METRIC EQUIVALENTS

MEASURES OF LENGTH

1 Inch=(72 points or 12 lines)=2.54 centimetres
12 Inches=1 foot=30.48 centimetres
3 Feet=1 yard (36 inches)=.914399 metres
5½ Yards=1 rod, pole or perch=5.0292 metres
4 Poles (22 yards)=1 chain=20.116 metres
10 Chains (40 poles)=1 furlong=2.0016 hektometres
8 Furlongs=1 mile=1760 yards=5280 feet=1.6903 kilometres

CUBIC MEASURE

1 Cubic Inch=16.388 cubic centimetres
1728 Cubic Inches=1 cubic foot=28.318 cubic decimetres
27 Cubic Feet=1 cubic yard=.7645 cubic metre

SQUARE OR SURFACE MEASURE

1 Square Inch=6.4516 square centimetres
144 Squar Inches=1 square foot=929.03 square centimetres
9 Square Feet=1 square yard=.8361 square metres
30¼ Square Yards=1 rod, pole or perch=25.292 square metres
40 Poles or perches=1 rood=10.1168 square dekametres
4 Roods (4840 sq. yards)=1 acre=40.4472 square dekametres
640 Acres (2560 roods)=6400 chains=3,097,600 sq. yards=1 sq. mile=2.5885 sq. kilometres.

AVOIRDUPOIS WEIGHT

1 Dram=1.772 grams
16 Drams (437½ grains)=1 ounce (oz.)=28.352 grams
16 Ounces (7000 grains)=1 pound (lb.)=4.536 hectograms
14 Pounds=1 stone (st.)=6.35 kilograms
28 Pounds=1 quarter (qr.)=12.7 kilograms
4 Quarters (112 lbs.=1 hundredweight (cwt.)=50.8 kilograms
20 Hundredweights (2240 lbs.)=1 ton=1.016 metric tons

TROY WEIGHT

1 Grain=.0648 gram
24 Grains=1 pennyweight (dwt.)=1.5552 grams
20 Pennyweights=1 ounce (oz.)=31.104 grams
12 Ounces=1 pound=373.248 grams

CONVERSION OF BRITISH AND METRIC MEASURES

To Convert	Multiply by
Inches to Centimetres	2.540
Centimetres to Inches	0.3937
Feet to Metres	0.3048
Metres to Feet	3.281
Yards to Metres	0.9144
Metres to Yards	1.094
Miles to Kilometres	1.609
Kilometres to Miles	0.6214
Square Inches to Square Centimetres	6.452

Respect a man he will do the more.

CALENDAR for 1955

	JANUARY	FEBRUARY	MARCH	APRIL	MAY	JUNE
S	-2 9 16 23 30	... 6 13 20 27	... 6 13 20 27	... 3 10 17 24	1 8 15 22 29	... 5 12 19 26
M	-3 10 17 24 31	... 7 14 21 28	... 7 14 21 28	... 4 11 18 25	2 9 16 23 30	... 6 13 20 27
Tu	-4 11 18 25 ...	1 8 15 22 ...	1 8 15 22 29	... 5 12 19 26	3 10 17 24 31	... 7 14 21 28
W	-5 12 19 26 ...	2 9 16 23 ...	2 9 16 23 30	... 6 13 20 27	4 11 18 25 ...	1 8 15 22 29
Th	-6 13 20 27 ...	3 10 17 24 ...	3 10 17 24 31	... 7 14 21 28	5 12 19 26 ...	2 9 16 23 30
F	-7 14 21 28 ...	4 11 18 25 ...	4 11 18 25 ...	1 8 15 22 29	6 13 20 27 ...	3 10 17 24 ...
S	1 8 15 22 29	5 12 19 26 ...	5 12 19 26 ...	2 9 16 23 30	7 14 21 28 ...	4 11 18 25 ...

	JULY	AUGUST	SEPTEMBER	OCTOBER	NOVEMBER	DECEMBER
S	-3 10 17 24 31	... 7 14 21 28	... 4 11 18 25	-2 9 16 23 30	... 6 13 20 27	... 4 11 18 25
M	-4 11 18 25 ...	1 8 15 22 29	... 5 12 19 26	-3 10 17 24 31	... 7 14 21 28	... 5 12 19 26
Tu	-5 12 19 26 ...	2 9 16 23 30	... 6 13 20 27	-4 11 18 25 ...	1 8 15 22 29	... 6 13 20 27
W	-6 13 20 27 ...	3 10 17 24 31	... 7 14 21 28	-5 12 19 26 ...	2 9 16 23 30	... 7 14 21 28
Th	-7 14 21 28 ...	4 11 18 25 ...	1 8 15 22 29	-6 13 20 27 ...	3 10 17 24 ...	1 8 15 22 29
F	1 8 15 22 29	5 12 19 26 ...	2 9 16 23 30	-7 14 21 28 ...	4 11 18 25 ...	2 9 16 23 30
S	2 9 16 23 30	6 13 20 27 ...	3 10 17 24 ...	1 8 15 22 29	5 12 19 26 ...	3 10 17 24 31

CALENDAR for 1954

	JANUARY	FEBRUARY	MARCH	APRIL	MAY	JUNE
S	-3 10 17 24 31	... 7 14 21 28	... 7 14 21 28	... 4 11 18 25	-2 9 16 23 30	... 6 13 20 27
M	-4 11 18 25 ...	1 8 15 22 ...	1 8 15 22 29	... 5 12 19 26	-3 10 17 24 31	... 7 14 21 28
Tu	-5 12 19 26 ...	2 9 16 23 ...	2 9 16 23 30	... 6 13 20 27	-4 11 18 25 ...	1 8 15 22 29
W	-6 13 20 27 ...	3 10 17 24 ...	3 10 17 24 31	... 7 14 21 28	-5 12 19 26 ...	2 9 16 23 30
Th	-7 14 21 28 ...	4 11 18 25 ...	4 11 18 25 ...	1 8 15 22 29	-6 13 20 27 ...	3 10 17 24 ...
F	1 8 15 22 29	5 12 19 26 ...	5 12 19 26 ...	2 9 16 23 30	-7 14 21 28 ...	4 11 18 25 ...
S	2 9 16 23 30	6 13 20 27 ...	6 13 20 27 ...	3 10 17 24 ...	1 8 15 22 29	5 12 19 26 ...

	JULY	AUGUST	SEPTEMBER	OCTOBER	NOVEMBER	DECEMBER
S	... 4 11 18 25	1 8 15 22 29	... 5 12 19 26	-3 10 17 24 31	... 7 14 21 28	... 5 12 19 26
M	... 5 12 19 26	2 9 16 23 30	... 6 13 20 27	-4 11 18 25 ...	1 8 15 22 29	... 6 13 20 27
Tu	... 6 13 20 27	3 10 17 24 31	... 7 14 21 28	-5 12 19 26 ...	2 9 16 23 30	... 7 14 21 28
W	... 7 14 21 28	4 11 18 25 ...	1 8 15 22 29	-6 13 20 27 ...	3 10 17 24 ...	1 8 15 22 29
Th	1 8 15 22 29	5 12 19 26 ...	2 9 16 23 30	-7 14 21 28 ...	4 11 18 25 ...	2 9 16 23 30
F	2 9 16 23 30	6 13 20 27 ...	3 10 17 24 ...	1 8 15 22 29	5 12 19 26 ...	3 10 17 24 31
S	3 10 17 24 31	7 14 21 28 ...	4 11 18 25 ...	2 9 16 23 30	6 13 20 27 ...	4 11 18 25 ...

CALENDAR for 1953

	JANUARY	FEBRUARY	MARCH	APRIL	MAY	JUNE
S	... 4 11 18 25	1 8 15 22 ...	1 8 15 22 29	... 5 12 19 26	-3 10 17 24 31	... 7 14 21 28
M	... 5 12 19 26	2 9 16 23 ...	2 9 16 23 30	... 6 13 20 27	-4 11 18 25 ...	1 8 15 22 29
Tu	... 6 13 20 27	3 10 17 24 ...	3 10 17 24 31	... 7 14 21 28	-5 12 19 26 ...	2 9 16 23 30
W	... 7 14 21 28	4 11 18 25 ...	4 11 18 25 ...	1 8 15 22 29	-6 13 20 27 ...	3 10 17 24 ...
Th	1 8 15 22 29	5 12 19 26 ...	5 12 19 26 ...	2 9 16 23 30	-7 14 21 28 ...	4 11 18 25 ...
F	2 9 16 23 30	6 13 20 27 ...	6 13 20 27 ...	3 10 17 24 ...	1 8 15 22 29	5 12 19 26 ...
S	3 10 17 24 31	7 14 21 28 ...	7 14 21 28 ...	4 11 18 25 ...	2 9 16 23 30	6 13 20 27 ...

	JULY	AUGUST	SEPTEMBER	OCTOBER	NOVEMBER	DECEMBER
S	... 5 12 19 26	-2 9 16 23 30	... 6 13 20 27	... 4 11 18 25	1 8 15 22 29	... 6 13 20 27
M	... 6 13 20 27	-3 10 17 24 31	... 7 14 21 28	... 5 12 19 26	2 9 16 23 30	... 7 14 21 28
Tu	... 7 14 21 28	-4 11 18 25 ...	1 8 15 22 29	... 6 13 20 27	3 10 17 24 ...	1 8 15 22 29
W	1 8 15 22 29	-5 12 19 26 ...	2 9 16 23 30	... 7 14 21 28	4 11 18 25 ...	2 9 16 23 30
Th	2 9 16 23 30	-6 13 20 27 ...	3 10 17 24 ...	1 8 15 22 29	5 12 19 26 ...	3 10 17 24 31
F	3 10 17 24 31	-7 14 21 28 ...	4 11 18 25 ...	2 9 16 23 30	6 13 20 27 ...	4 11 18 25 ...
S	4 11 18 25 ...	1 8 15 22 29	5 12 19 26 ...	3 10 17 24 31	7 14 21 28 ...	5 12 19 26 ...

PARTY GAMES

NOISES OFF: Give your guests pencil and paper and have them seated. From behind a screen or in any spot where you will not be seen by your guests but can be heard, you proceed to make certain noises which they try to identify and write down on their paper.

Before the party starts you have all your props ready in a suitcase. Here are some of the noises which you can make (and although very evident to you sometimes they are not so clear from the other side of a screen): Grating a carrot; blowing up a balloon or paper bag; using a ratchet screwdriver; brushing your teeth; tinkling your keys—and many other noises which you will discover.

THE DRAWING GAME: Divide your party into teams with a maximum number of 12 in the team. Each team should be gathered around a small table on which there is a writing pad and pencil. You stand at the other end of the room with a list of prepared clues, which, in this instance, we will say are song titles.

Each team chooses a representative who move in your direction and from you will receive a song title, which they must try to describe in a drawing. You must whisper the title so that none of the others in their team hear it. They then rush back to the pad on their own table and proceed with the drawing.

A simple one, for instance, " Tea for Two," where two tea-cups would make it easily identifiable, or " Yes, we have no bananas," " Horsey, keep your tail up," " Daisy, Daisy." And then you can go on to the slightly more difficult ones like " Roamin' in the Gloamin'," "London's Burning," " John Brown's Body."

The person chosen to do the drawing must not use any letters or figures and must answer no questions of his team or give them the slightest verbal indication as to what he is attempting to draw. As the team is watching their artist they must call out whatever song title they think is the clue. Whenever you hear the correct clue you award that team a point. Then each team chooses another artist, and so on until all have had a chance to show their skill.

This game can be both fascinating and hilarious, but you must keep up the pace. For instance, much will depend on the speed the artist moves from you to his table.

PASSING THE BALL: A very informal game. Arrange two teams facing one another, and alternate men and women. Pass a tennis ball (or a lemon or an orange would do instead) along the team by transferring it from neck to neck. It is quite easy to hold it under the chin but not so easy to pass it to one's neighbour without touching it with your hands. If the ball is dropped it must be returned to the beginning of the line. The first line to get a ball to the end wins.

Instead of " Passing the Ball," it can be just as hilarious to use the outside of a match box passing it from nose to nose without the use of hands.

There are two sides to every question.

WHERE ARE YOU? A grand game for the young people. Participants take hands and form a big circle. Two people go into the centre, blindfolded, and each is given a magazine or newspaper tightly rolled and tied to form a truncheon. One tries to hit the other and each player indicates his position by saying " I'm here!" Each time this is said, the other player gives one hit.

When a player is hit, a change is made, and two others go to the centre.

VERY TASTY: Several girls are standing, well spaced out, and opposite to them, at a distance of several yards, the same number of men, blindfolded. Each has a small piece of chocolate in his hand (or instead of chocolate, caramel, or, preferably, a piece of soft fruit like a strawberry). He has to go forward and try to pop it into his partner's mouth. The first person to achieve this is the winner—and he deserves some reward, perhaps a chocolate for himself!

Alternatively: Blindfold the girls. Give each a little baking tin with a small quantity of potato crisps, and a teaspoon. They have to feed the men.

HITTING THE ORANGE: This game to be played in pairs and, if numbers permit, three pairs to take part at once.

Each player to be given in his right hand a spoon with an orange (or tennis ball) on it. In the left hand he holds another spoon. His aim is to knock off his opponent's orange whilst keeping his own on the spoon.

Have several heats and afterwards let the winners play one another.

IN THE MANNER OF THE WORD: Choose one of your guests, who should select a partner and leave the room. The rest of the party should then decide on an adverb—madly, nicely, coyly, daintily, etc.

The couple then return and can approach any of the party and suggest that they do some familiar task "In the Manner of the Word."

Presume that the word chosen by the team is " Coyly." Well, they can suggest to a gentleman that he brushes the fireplace In the Manner of the Word. Or, a lady might be approached and she asked to speak to her grocer on the telephone In the Manner of the Word. Another gent. might be asked to choose a lady and propose to her In the Manner of the Word.

Now, if you can imagine all these things being done " Coyly," then you get some idea of the fun that can be created. After each little performance the couple can then suggest two adverbs before asking the next person to perform the act.

Alternative to " In the Manner of the Word "—

ADVERBS: This game is suitable for half-a-dozen to twenty players. One member, who later becomes the Questioner, withdraws from the group whilst the others hold their consultation.

Joy often comes after sorrow like morning after night.

They fix upon an adverb which they will indicate by the manner in which they answer the questions put to them. Suppose they have chosen " disagreeably," each player on being questioned must answer in a disagreeable manner. When the Questioner has guessed the adverb, another player takes a turn.

The next adverb might be " joyously," the next " briefly," then " dramatically," " sarcastically," " untruthfully," " shyly," and so on. Sometimes the demeanour of the players will indicate the word and sometimes, as in the case of " untruthfully," the actual wording of the answers. There is scope for much variety in this game.

SOLO ACT: Send eight people out of the room. The remaining people then decide some everyday occurrence which they must act one by one. There must be no words or props.

The success of this game depends upon the type of activity which they decide should be enacted. There should always be a certain amount of movement but nothing too obvious.

" Bathing baby and changing its nappy " has become a bit too monotonous. So try and be more original. Here are some suggestions: (1) Presume you are the guard on a train. Watch the passengers board the train at the last minute. Then look at your vest pocket watch. After which you move down the platform closing the carriage doors. Turn round and blow your whistle. Wave your flag, pause, then jump into the guard's van a second or two later. (2) Presume you are a grocer attending to a customer who wants some bacon. You show her the first ham, which doesn't please her. Then you show her a second ham, which presumably she likes. You then put the ham on the machine, swinging the handle and the various slices fall on the paper. Then you take the ham in the paper to the weighing machine, finding it short you go back and do another slice. Parcel it, accept the money, and smile.

CHARADES: A charade consists in the presentation of the syllables of a word separately, and then the whole word. The old notion was to have any sort of scene and to say the word a number of times during the course of it. A more interesting method is to let the scene be a fair representation of the idea for which the word stands. This gives more aim and purpose to each scene, and it is not vital for the audience to listen for every word of the conversation. In fact, one or more of the scenes may be presented in dumb show, if it is thought advisable.

When choosing charade words, select those that are composed of two or more definite and colourful words, so that the audience have a fair chance of guessing. There is no point in choosing a word made up of insignificant syllables.

Here are a few useful words: Ham-let, buoy-ant, chair-man, scar-let, car-case, hurri-cane, law-suit, moon-light, news-paper, pack-age, sky-lark, watch-man, Sun-day, butter-fly, fare-well, work-house, sel-fish, man-sion, mis-chief, peni-tent, wish-bone, fan-atic, underground, sand-wiches, con-sump-tion.

Blessings are not valued until they are gone.

GAMES FOR A SMALL PARTY

FISHING FOR BUTTONS: Have a good-sized bowl of buttons and let four competitors at a time fish for them with a bent pin on a piece of string.

FISHING FOR RICE: Have as many saucers of rice as there are competitors. The object is to pick up with two knitting needles as many grains of rice as possible in two minutes.

MATCHBOX CONTEST: Put a few matches into a box and let competitors shake the box in turn and record their guess. There will be wide variations in the number estimated.

PIN PUSHING: Give each competitor a cake of soap and a saucer of tiny pins. The object is to push as many pins into the soap as possible within the space of half a minute.

FUNNY FACES: The " victims " stand in a row facing the rest of the party. They are then asked to register various emotions—love, hate, simplicity, craftiness, grief, joy, fear, jealousy, anger, etc. The audience vote for the one they think the most successful.

GOING ON HOLIDAY: A memory game: "A" says: " I'm going on holiday and am taking with me . . . " (stating the name of an article). " B " repeats the same sentence, saying "A's" article and adding another. The game continues—a fresh article being added to the list each time—until the memory of one of the players breaks down.
